AF228126

THE
CALLING

DEAN C. GARDNER

This book is dedicated to my son, the good doctor.

Contents

SECTION 1

Movement of presence

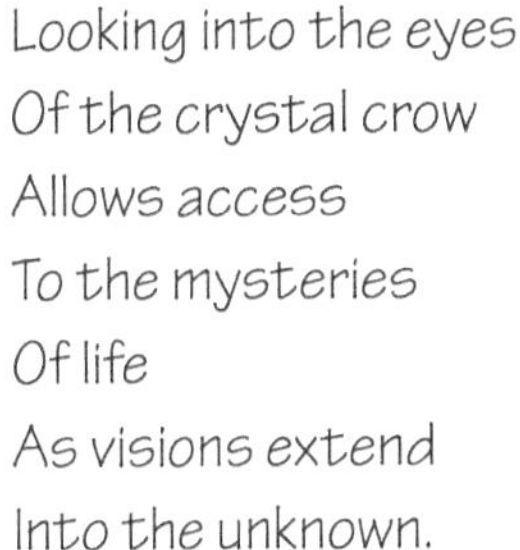

Looking into the eyes
Of the crystal crow
Allows access
To the mysteries
Of life
As visions extend
Into the unknown.

Feeling the presence
Of the way, the Truth
And the life
I unearth the purpose
Of being toward Truth
As the living moment
Triggers service
To The Unknown God.

Then pure music
Fills my heart
With joy and wonder.

Then
The scarlet rose
Dances dreams
Across my landscape
As a leap of faith
Takes me
Into the house
Of many mansions.

It is from here
That The Spirit of Wisdom
Speaks to my soul.

There is no greater
Mystery in life
Than the love
Of The Unknown God.

*

There is life
In these old bones
As I face the altar
Of The Unknown God.

For seven decades
And more
I proceeded in this world
With a faith
That always returned
To the way, the Truth
And the life.

Finding treasures
In endless possibility
I have unearthed
Purpose., as I salute
The Spirit of Wisdom

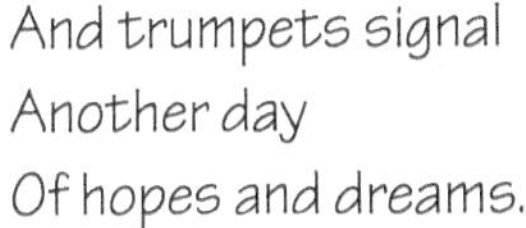

And trumpets signal
Another day
Of hopes and dreams.

I have seen
The light in the eyes
Of my grandchildren
And they have awakened
Love in my heart.

My son and I talk
About the relevance
Of the other side
Of the sky
And my daughter-in-law
Dresses herself with kindness.

So, I am thankful
For these gifts
As I continue on.

*

It is
The first snow
And drifts
Of beauty blanket
The roads with purity.

As I drive
Through the darkness
There is no trace
Of dawn.

In my spot
With a cup of coffee
I hear the old veterans
Weave laughter
Into hunting stories
As their lives bare
Good times only.

They are
Survivors facing
The elements
With undaunted courage.

Their blood speaks
Freedom
Into the living moment
As life echoes

Truth
Into the dawn
Of a first snow.

*

Driving through the snow
Slip sliding my way
I see hope in the darkness
As the cold encompasses
All and everything.

Feeling the presence
Of The Spirit of Wisdom
Approach
My mind reaches
Into the other side
Of time and space
As I travel the road
To eternity.

I head North
Through the snow
To my son's home
Where family brews
Love into the living
Moment.

As I arrive quiet falls
Upon the earth
Until I hear
Their pure music
Releasing the peace
Beyond understanding.

To dwell
In what matters
I find the love
Of family.

*

It is early
And the old men
Gather
Over a cup of coffee.

Where I sit
There is no tomorrow
As my heart follows
The rhythm
Of the universe
Into the unknown.

Then
The sun rises
And it is
Tomorrow.

Standing
On the edge
Of eternity
I see
Through a looking

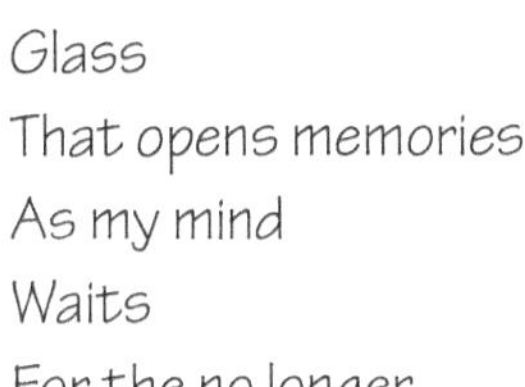

Glass
That opens memories
As my mind
Waits
For the no longer.

When I look
Into the mirror
I wonder whose face
Appears so old.

*

Walking toward death
The long days
Bending time
I watch the years
Bury the man who I was.

The ache
Pushing my mind
Into orbits
Around the here and now
Forms a promise
Of the nearness
To joy and wonder.

I listen
To pure music
Take my heart
Into the no longer
As I count
My footsteps
To forevermore.

The journey is over
And the destination
Blossoms.

As my grandchildren
Play in the yard
I step into my grave.

I will not
Cheat death
Any longer.

*

When young
I climbed cliffs
For fun.

How I lived
Through those adventures
I do not know.

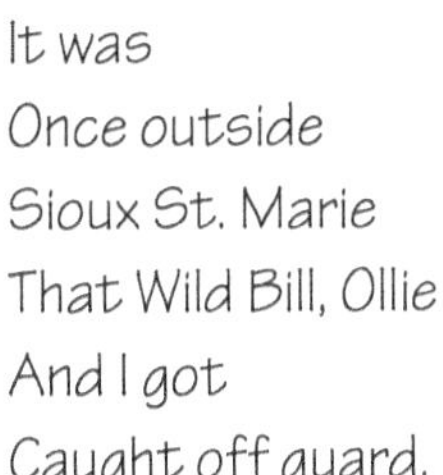

It was
Once outside
Sioux St. Marie
That Wild Bill, Ollie
And I got
Caught off guard.

Wild Bill was
A geology student
And Ollie was
His dog.

We were on
Our way to Ottawa
When we saw
Some cliffs
To the left.

I made it to the top
With Wild Bill's help
But he was stranded
On a ledge.

Two Indian boys
Heard our cries
For help
On their way home
From fishing.

Now
I am challenged
By climbing the stairs.

Getting old gets that way
But my spirit carries on.

*

There were
Three of us in the sixties.

Tom was a visual artist
Painting absurdity
In black and white
While Jack was
A musician with dreams
Of being a rock star
And then there was me.

We bonded together
Wandering the back roads
Of the third coast.

Tom jumped off a bridge
To his death
On the interstate.

Jack hanged himself
In the basement
Of a mental hospital.

So
I was left to carry on
With a pocket of words.

*

It came to pass
That every Sunday
My eldest granddaughter
Baked sweet treats
For me
And I delighted
In the aroma sent
From her heart.

Caught in a dream
I see the beginning
Of a tradition
And this luscious scent
Awakens Sunday morning
To the world
Of smoking dragons.

The love from this child
Skyrockets my dreams

As my heart feels
The pure music
Of innocence.

Radiant, her blue eyes
Shower me with the light
From angelic places
Yet, she completes
My dreams
With the infusion
Of love
Only a child can give.

There is a delicate beauty
In her smile and I am
Thankful for her look.

*

Autumn leaves
Fill my casket
With the love
Of The Unknown God
Welcoming me
To the promised land.

I hear
The count
Center on zero.

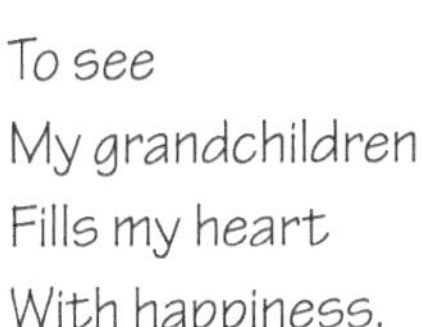

To see
My grandchildren
Fills my heart
With happiness.

With my son standing by
My daughter-in-law
By his side
We talk about
What matters.

So, there is Truth
In life
Written upon the heart
As we share time.

As my substance
Explores the unknown
My family weeps
On my gravestone.

*

In my library
A small room
In my apartment
A captain's chair
Dwells in one corner.

My grandfather sat on it
At his kitchen table.

I remember
Seeing him sit there
As he read his Bible.

That is the way
He died
Sitting on his
Captain's chair
Reading his Bible.

Although bookcases
Surround my library
There are boxes of books
Waiting to fill the room
With knowledge.

Looking out the window
That faces north
I count stars
In the night sky
With my grandfather's
Telescope.

I believe they are
The same stars
My grandfather saw.

I wonder
If he too counted them.

*

Early in the garden
Of tables and chairs
When darkness surrounds
The here and now
I believe my way
Into the light
Of one
Dimensional reality
And the thunder
Of thought echoes
Through the vitals
Of being toward Truth.

It is the will
Of my substance
That travels
Beyond space and time
Ever searching for Truth
And the authentic article
Of actuality.

It is
That matter expands
Into endless possibility

Through the constant
Of space:
space, the constitution
Of all and everything.

Having launched
From the garden
Of tables and chairs
I affirm the actuality
Of The Unknown God
As the primordial
Beginning
Based upon the evidence.

*

Feeling the proximity
Of the always already there
I configure the physics
Of being toward Truth
As a two-dimensional
Reality transforms
Then and there
Into the here and now.

It is the formulation
Of being in nothingness
Into the substance

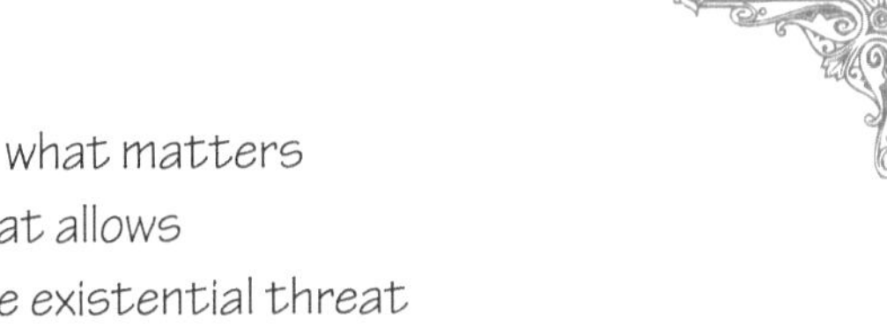

Of what matters
That allows
The existential threat
Of the no longer to be
As language defines
Endless possibility.

As the look
Of the crystal crow
Opens my inner eye
To the unknown
I travel through
A parabola of time
To connect my substance
With the calculus of hope.

Then, there is
An equation to Truth
Through the geometry
Of the mystery of life
As the mathematics
Of the always already
There configures
Pure music into being
Toward Truth.

Consequently, I worship
The Unknown God.

*

Following the flight
Of the crystal crow
Through the authentic article
I feel the energy
Of the always already there
And trumpets sound
At the presence of life
Liberty and the pursuit
Of happiness.

Stepping into the wilds
Of times and a half
I see the collapse
Of what matters
Although the crystal crow
Carries a remnant
To the land of promise.

Asa my substance pursues
The living moment
Where the light
Of one-dimensional
Reality creates pure music
I look to the way, the Truth
And the life for deliverance
From the abyss.

Then, the crystal crow
Speaks Truth
Into the here and now.

So, the crystal crow is my love
My life and my muse.

*

As the encompassing
Defines the movement
Of actuality
Into the here and now
My mind registers
The appearance
Of the authentic article
As the experiential.

It is a given
From the vertical
Column of time
That the living moment
Pyramids being toward Truth
Onto the thresholds
Of forevermore
As I march
Into the backlands
Of mind.

How my thoughts awaken
Through a looking
Glass to Truth.

How the inner eye
Of being toward Truth
Reveals the realities
Of the experiential.

How the optics
Of the experiential
Reflect the authentic article
From actuality.

It is good
To be alive
With pure music.

*

As the light
From a full moon
Emanates the presence
Of another reality
Where spirits ride
The rhythm of the universe
I look between the lines
Written on a wall
Of silence.

There, among the bones
Of Truth
The mystery of life

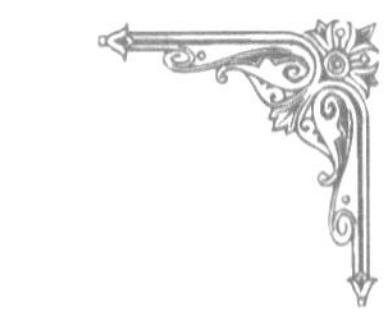

Staggers the mind
Passing it into the abyss
Until pure music
Trumpets thought
From the graves
Of the here and now.

I see in the shadows
The movement of spirits
From another reality
As I seek the purpose
Of what matters.

Then, the moon speaks
Truth into the muscle
Of mind
As spirits dance
To the drums of eternity
And I step into the light
Of one-dimensional
Reality.

So, there is purpose
In the blood
Of being toward Truth.

*

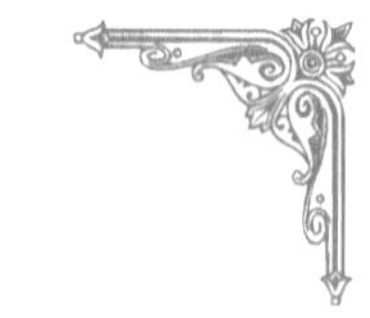

As pure music triggers
My heart with passion
My mind follows
The rhythm of the universe
Onto the way, the Truth
And the life.

Visions of the other sided
Of time and space
Occupy being toward Truth
With the language
Of the authentic article
As The Spirit of Wisdom
Calls me to one
Dimensional reality.

Looking through
The mirror of thought
My inner eye opens
To the splendor
Of The Unknown God
And the crystal crow
Dances across the sky
With pure music.

In that living moment
The presence
Of being toward Truth
Climbs out of self
And the deep touch

Moves me into the peace
Beyond understanding.

*

Riding the rhythm
Of the universe
To unite with the crystal crow
Leads to life, liberty
And the pursuit of happiness
As The Spirit of Wisdom
Clears the mind
And purifies the heart.

Witnessing the beauty
Of pure music allows
Time present to launch
Into the mystery of life
As visions of the always
Already there explode
Into the face
Of the celestial clocks.

So, I look into the mirror
Of time and space.

So, I reflect upon
The presence of the actual.

So, the substance
Of the beyond embraces
Being toward Truth
With the deep touch.

Then, the crystal crow
Carries my thought
Into endless possibility.

Then, my substance smiles.

*

In the land of the crystal crow
Thoughts lead to the peace
Beyond understanding
As mind rests in the passion
Of bliss.

Surrounded by the treasures
Of the always already there
Being toward Truth
Pursues life
Into the living moment
And I bask in the beauty
Of the other side
Of time and space.

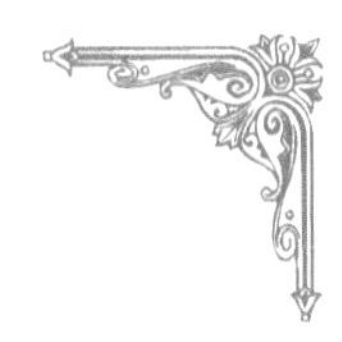

Then, hopes and dreams
Become visions
Leading to freedom.

Then, being toward Truth
Grasps the mystery of life.

So, I walk with the faith
In the way, the Truth
And the life
Onto forevermore.

SECTION 2

Collision of time in space

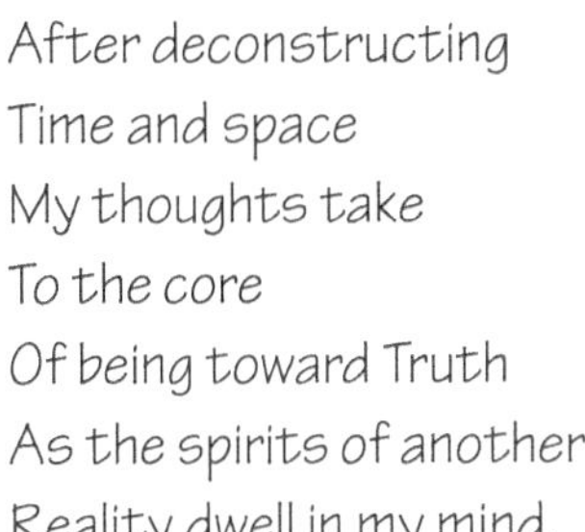

After deconstructing
Time and space
My thoughts take
To the core
Of being toward Truth
As the spirits of another
Reality dwell in my mind.

Then, in the darkness
Of oblivion, I penetrate
The stronghold of being
And nothingness
And the tyranny
Of existential threats
Crumble.

It is The Spirit of Wisdom
That establishes
A house of many mansions
Into the here and now
While I bask In the presence
Of one-dimensional
Reality.

Occupied by the rhythm
Of the universe
My heart feels its way
Out of oblivion
And onto the substance
Of what matters.

Then, pure music
Choreographs the danced
Of the crystal crow
And I witness the birth
Of Truth.

*

Unearthing the archeology
Of presence, I place my trust
In the way, the Truth
And the life
As the wind speaks
With the language
Of The Spirit of Wisdom.

After carving the rock
Of my tombstone
I place the monument
Of my life in the footsteps
Leading to one
Dimensional reality.

Then, a hard rain falls
From the darkness
And time measures
The will of being
Toward Truth.

Then, the crystal crow knocks
At my chamber door
And I remember that I too
Was vital in the land
Of the free and brave.

So, I close my eyes
And fall asleep
In Abraham's bosom.

*

Tapping
Into the brainwaves
From the other side
Of time and space
I gather the image
Of the crystal crow
Circling the presence
Of my being toward Truth.

The substance that it
Carried altered the reality
That I lived in
As hope replaced absurdity.

Although I once dwelt
In a purposeless world
Where nothing made sense

The Spirit of Wisdom fed
My mind, speaking through
The crystal crow.

Then, there was the flow
Of pure music that defined
The doctrine of the landscape
From the always already
There in the presence
Of The Unknown God.

So, I understood that the way
The Truth and the life
Is the primordial source
Of being toward Truth.

*

In my library there is
A moon that lights
The mystery of life
As my mind opens
To endless possibility.

In the background
Pure music infuses me
With visions beyond
The here and now
As thoughts orbit

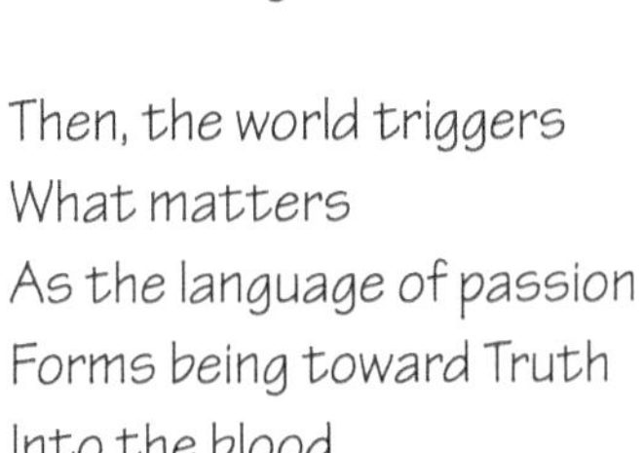

Around being
And nothingness.

Then, the world triggers
What matters
As the language of passion
Forms being toward Truth
Into the blood
Of the living moment.

The awakening of mind
To the trumpets
Of one-dimensional
Reality takes my want
Into mountains of promise
And there, the treasures
Of life, liberty, and the pursuit
Of happiness feed need.

Then, the moon in my library
Conveys The Spirit of Wisdom
To enlighten the shadows
Of what I am.

*

As the threat
Of outliving myself
Looms across my brain

I step into the rhythm
Of the universe
And destiny carries me
Onto being toward Truth

Among the wounds
That harvest pain
I see my purpose
Fade across thoughts
As my heart pounds with hope.

It is that the living moment
Calls me to journey
Into the unknown
As my mind stalls
In moments of silence.

Seeking the pure music
Of the way, the Truth
And the life, I look
For The Spirit of Wisdom
To feed my hunger
With promise.

Then, a song touches my heart.

Then, I feel the presence
Of The Unknown God.

Then, I step into the beyond
With visions of the always
Already there.

So, with the rebirth of purpose
I carry on.

*

In the cold of times
I search the sky
For the crystal crow
And time withers
My mind.

As decades bury thought
My mind yearns
For a connection to what
is greater than what I am.

Then, the crystal crow
Brings the dawn
Of being toward Truth
And I purpose myself
Into the substance
Of what matters.

The cold is not so cold
As I endure the present

And hope my way
Into time future.

Then, the crystal crow
Points to The Unknown God
Before me
And the warmth
Of blessed assurance
Caresses my cheek.

It is good to endure.

*

As pure music permeates
The air, I tumble
Into the arms of love
And the mystery of life
Dances in my mind.

There is the swarming
Of thoughts that detach
The here and now
From the living moment
And I find my heart
Keeping to the rhythm
Of the universe.

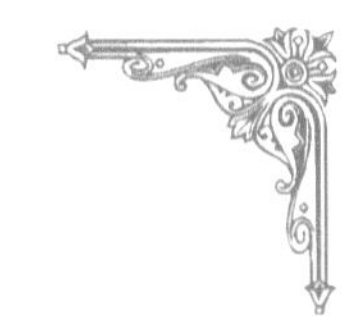

So, my thoughts take me
Into a dream
Where light penetrates
The shadows of being
And time.

Then, the celestial clocks
Take me into rivers of song
And I brave the unknown.

As I live in a two
Dimensional reality
I picture the love
Of The Unknown God.

Then, the drums
Of eternity eclipse
Being toward Truth
And I emerge
Through the embrace
Of pure music.

*

Through the flight
Of the crystal crow
Mind travels beyond
The horizon of the here
And now onto the always
Already there.

Crashing through the linear
Thought advances
Into endless possibility
As pure music pyramids
From the one-dimensional
Reality and the crystal crow
Speaks the language of love
From The Unknown God.

So, I listen to the message
From the crystal crow
Imparting Truth in the words
Of The Spirit of Wisdom.

Then, my inner eye sees
The work of the mystery
Of life and the fearsome symmetry
Of being toward Truth
Conquers all doubt.

Although time threatens
My walk-in faith
The way, the Truth

And the life
Steady my course.

*

In the silence
Of the unspoken word
Dreams carry thought
Beyond the here and now
To endless possibility.

Although want howls
Across the terrain
Of emptiness
Need reaches
Into the substance
Of what matters
And a song loosens
The tongue of being
Toward Truth.

Then, my mind slips
Into the light
Of the everlasting
And the drums of eternity
Carry my heart
To the other side
Of being in nothingness.

It is the will to power
That covers what matters
As I look in the mirror
And see silence cover
The living moment.

Although my thoughts find
Meaning between lines
Of hope, the mystery of life
Speaks the language of silence.

*

As dreams of today
Covers the snows
Of tomorrow
Mind penetrates the unknown
With vigor
And thoughts carry me
Into the times
Of the celestial clocks.

Traveling beyond the here
And now my heart
Liberates me from darkness.

Exploding into time
And space, mind deconstructs
The legacy of being in time

As the moment pictures
Illusions of being there.

It is when being toward Truth
Reaches into what matters
That I feel the movement
Of an epiphany
In the living moment.

So, the snow of what
Is there dresses
The landscape in wonder.

So, my heart feels
The beauty of the here
And now that leads
To the always
Already there.

*

Chasing ghosts across the snow
The crystal crow captures
The drift of cold.

Frozen in the living moment
Time grows icicles
In the brain
As thoughts slip into dreams.

Looking across blankets
Of white, I see
The crystal crow writes
My destiny
Into time and space
As the forum of forevermore
Buries the cold into life.

Among the deep freeze
Of times and a half
The crystal crow carries
My load
Out of the shadows
As sweat turns
Into frozen tears.

Then, I curl around
The fire pits
Imagining the domain
Of Truth.

Then, the warmth of pure music
Delivers visions of forevermore.

So, I walk through the snow
In the footsteps of the way
The Truth and the life.

*

Centered upon drifts of cold
The crystal crow gathers
Times and a half into treasures
Of thought as my heart
Follows the rhythm
Of the universe.

Then, visions form
Around a song
As the wind gusts
In bursts of cold.

Then, icicles grow
Across my brain
And feeling the cold
Carries the want
For an embrace
Of warmth.

To be alive in the living
Moment allows me
To pyramid into pure music
As the crystal crow
Calls me out of the freeze.

As the crystal crow
Feeds into want
My mind looks to spring
When the song of flowers
Blossoms.

So, the crystal crow
My muse
Speaks the promise
Of seasons to pass in time.

So, the smile of the crystal crow
Keeps my heart warm and vital.

*

Warmed by the love in eternity
I listen to The Spirit of Wisdom
Pour pure music into my heart.

As the eternal light
Dwells in the peace
Beyond understanding
I took to the way
The Truth and the life
And blessed assurance
Pyramids me into the freedom
Of the living moment.

Then, I hear the trumpets
Of forevermore.

Then, a parade
Of the resurrection
Lights the heavenly bodies.

Emerging in a song
Being toward Truth
Eclipses time
And the living moment
Liberates me
From all constraint.

Pleading for no blame
Or shame, I am greeted
By a smile.

*

In one corner of my library
Stands a showcase
Made of mahogany
And stone glass.

An ivory angel releases
A dove carrying a message
To the four corners of the world
As the angel guards my treasures.

It is there among shadows
That I keep my visions
Lettered in blood.

How the earth of being
Toward Truth carries

Mountains of thought
As images of the beyond
Thrive in the shadows
Of my library.

How the living moment
Liberates the here and now
From bondage onto pure music
As the rhythm of the universe
Breathes a parabola of time
Kept by the celestial clocks.

So, the ivory angel
Dances in my dreams
As the one-dimensional
Reality anoints my sleep
With visions of eternity.

*

As the shadows of infamy
Threaten life and limb
With the temptations of trials
I look for the way, the Truth
And the life.

Thundering in my heart
A devastation saps
My life of blood

As I breathe the disgust
Of my demise.

Tragedy swamps my mind.

Terror drowns my thought.

Sinking deeper into the abyss
My eyes blister with pain.

Suddenly, I feel my faith
In The Unknown God
Deliver me into the peace
Beyond understanding
And my life rises
Into the light of the always
Already there.

So, there are no shadows
In the light of the one
Dimensional reality.

Through The Spirit of Wisdom
Being toward Truth
Blossoms with kisses
Of splendor forevermore.

*

From the center
Of being toward Truth
Mind launches
Into the unknown
As the mystery of life
Weaves a tapestry
On connectivity
To what matters.

As heart feels the way
To the other side
Of the living moment
Thoughts penetrate the myth
Of the here and now.

As I look into the eyes
Of the crystal crow
The abyss
Devours time present.

As I hear pure music
Chime from celestial clocks
The rhythm of the universe
Carries me into wonder
The other side of the abyss.

Although God and death
Remain mysteries of life
It is The Unknown God
That breathes life into my heart

And I am called to believe
In the way, the Truth,
And the life.

Then, I am liberated
From the prison
Of empty rhetoric
And The Spirit of Wisdom
Writes my life
Onto forevermore.

*

As the crystal crow
Circles being toward Truth
The here and now falls
Into echoes of what
I am and eternity embraces
The source of my substance.

Reaching beyond mind
My thoughts touch
The other side
Of time and space
As the shadows
Of dreams punctuate
What is there.

When I see
The light of the one

Dimensional reality
My mind is free
To travel through the unknown
As my inner eye opens
To a house of many mansions.

Then, the secrets held
By the mystery of life
Allow me to feel
The awesome wonders
Of the rhythm of the universe.

Then, I soar in a vertical
Column of time.

*

Coming out of dreams
Where visions stir
The mystery of life
 Into being toward Truth
My mind awakens
To life, liberty and the pursuit
Of happiness, as the rhythm
Of the universe penetrates
The living moment
With the anthem
Of Lady Liberty.

It is the pure music
Of rapture that takes
The sun out of darkness.

It is the cry of freedom
That brings breath
To the here and now.

Although the worlds attempts
To silence the voice
Of Lady Liberty
Shew pronounces the end
Of oppression.

Then, thoughts cancel
The empty rhetoric
Of the times
As being toward Truth
Is allowed to speak
With the language
Of The Spirit of Wisdom
And the children of promise
Rise with the wind of eternity
Carrying them into an epiphany.

*

Listening to the rhythm
Of the universe pour

Pure music into my heart
I open my inner eye
To endless possibility.

Then, the shadows of infamy
Cast a dense fog
Across the here and now
And mind hammers
The drums of eternity
To cancel the grip
Of the abyss.

There is a tension
Between seeing
What is there
And succumbing
To the oppression
Of adversity.

Then, the always already
There awakens my mind
With the blood
Of being toward Truth
And the crystal crow
Flies into the heart
Of what matters,

So, the will to be
Perseveres and the visions
Of the other side

Of the here and now
Triggers the breath of life.

*

Where the world conjures
Reality out of being there
Being toward Truth envisions
Actuality from the crystal crow.

As time present passes
Into a parabola of time
The gravity of what matters
Weighs upon mind
And thoughts hobble
From shadows.

Then, the dreams emanating
From the countenance at the source
Of being toward Truth
Register life, liberty
And the pursuit of happiness
And freedom grows
Into the doctrine of the landscape.

So, a two-dimensional reality
Becomes the process of perceiving
As Truth in the living moment
Orchestrates the will to be

And the breath carries pure music
Into revelation.

Aside from becoming there
The crystal crow, my muse
Speaks the language of The Spirit
Of Wisdom.

So, being toward Truth is
Continuously becoming there.

*

So, I have become a fictional
Character present in time and space
As the here and now
Writes the epitaph of my life.

Although I exist
Between the lines
Of my will to self-power
I feel the twilight
Of empty rhetoric
Spurning my hopes
And dreams.

Yearning to join
The Spirit of Wisdom
I stumble through words
That connect to nothingness.

Then, I feel the love
Of my grandchildren
And being toward Truth
Signs my legacy
In The Book of Life.

How awesome
The deep touch of love.

Then, the author of this text
Exits with the rhythm
Of the universe
Linking him
To the crystal crow, his muse.

Then, pure music emerges
From my silent heart.

*

As the thick of life
Meets the thin
Of being there
My heart runs low
And time drags.

Although it is the beginning
Of the end, I muscle
Life into being toward Truth

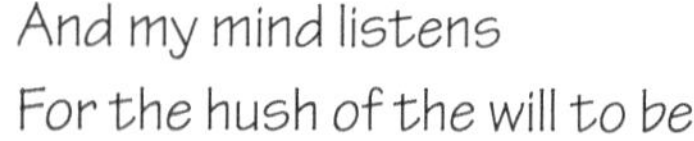

And my mind listens
For the hush of the will to be.

The look of death
Equips me with the faith
In the way, the Truth
And the life
And I come to terms
With the no longer.

Filling my time
With pure music
I gather thoughts
And a remnant
Of what I called myself
Smiles in the face
Of the everlasting.

The struggle nearly over
I treasure the peace
Beyond understanding
Holding this living moment
As a beginning.

So, the rhyme of death
Is silence.

*

It is from the beyond
That Truth is born
Into the air as the will
Of The Spirit of Wisdom
And pure music fills
The encompassing
With promise.

Although the flight
Of the crystal crow
Weighs the essence
Of being toward Truth
The world tries to abort Truth
But the will to be carries on
Through the rhythm
Of the universe.

So, I tend to the garden
Of mind.

As linear time opens
Endless possibility
Truth defines the living moment
As I purpose myself
Into the doctrine
Of the landscape.

So, the one
Dimensional reality
Beams the mystery

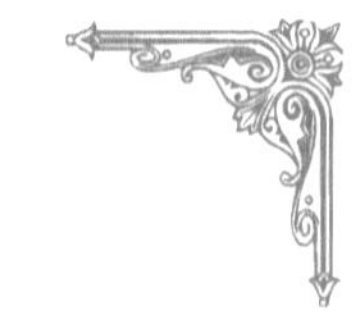

Of life into the here
And now and I listen
To the rhythm
Of the universe feed
The living moment
With treasure.

Thankful that my life is pyramided
To serve The Unknown God.

*

At the very moment
When I faced
Being in nothingness
The rhythm of the universe
Infused me with visions.

It was a matter of seeing
The darkness in shadows
And looking to the light.

It was a matter of undressing
The unknown and reaching
For one-dimensional reality.

Although the mystery
Of life covered the reality
Of being there

The actuality of being
Toward Truth proved
To be the birth
Of mind at the threshold
Of thought
And an image appeared
As the valley of dry bones.

Then, the crystal crow
Brought mana
From the way, the Truth
And the life
As pure music enlightened
The self that I knew.

Then, the peace
Beyond understanding
Filled me with awe
In the land of milk
And honey.

*

Off in the distance
Beyond many a horizon
Laughter creased
The living moment.

It was a sinister laugh
That brought tears
Across the face
Of being toward Truth
As a deep ache throttled me.

Then, the image of death
Awakened to the here
And now as time left
No trace of reason.

It was not the fear
Of death that pained me
But the loss of a connection
To loved ones.

So, death is a mystery
Of life and the fear
Of the unknown
Can cripple life.

Then, I took my mind
Into hope and trust
In the way, the Truth
And the life.

Death is not to be feared
But embraced as a new beginning
Where the unknown is known.

Then, the ache of being there
Disappeared and fear yielded
To the love of The Unknown God.

So, the here and now
Is there
To celebrate the love
Of The Unknown God.

*

It is that the crystal crow
Takes me into being
Toward Truth as the journey
Into the mystery of life
Opens my third eye
To what matters.

Connected to the authentic
Article I face I the here and now
With life, liberty
And the pursuit of happiness
As the doctrine of the landscape.

Connected to the rhythm
Of the universe, I launch
Into actuality, leaving
The constraints
Of reality as the celestial
Clocks trigger my will to be.

It is the crystal crow
That summons the deep touch
From the other side
Of the here and now
As a parabola of time
Pictures pure music
In my mind.

Then, I embrace the other side
Of time and space forevermore.

Although facts lead to evidence
In order to make a decision
Truth is a leap from there
Into the presence
Of The Spirit of Wisdom.

*

After drifting in time
And space the inner eye sees
The crystal crow
As the messenger
From The Unknown God
And heart feels the climax
Of the authentic article.

Because darkness shrouds
The living moment

With being there
Mind gathers the here
And now from the graveyard
Of the lost.

Grabbed by the will to be
The mind pictures the pure music
Of the crystal crow
After being toward Truth
Was staggered
By the oppressive loss.

It is The Spirit of Wisdom
That gathers eternal light
Feeding mind
With victory over despair.

Then, the crystal crow
Writes true love
As the destiny
Of being toward Truth
With the blood
Of forevermore.

*

So, space is infinite
And time is eternal.

So, being exists
But nothingness does not exist
Except as it weighs upon the heart
As dread.

So, a three-dimensional reality
Is the dwelling place
Of the will to be
As a linear actuality.

So, a two-dimensional reality
Is the calculus of images
Of thought existing
As a parabola of time.

So, one-dimensional reality
Is the architecture of the always
Already there
As a vertical column of time.

Listening to pure music
I step outside myself
And enter a two
Dimensional reality
As mind connects
To being toward Truth.

Then, my will to be
Rides the rhythm
Of the universe

Since I am liberated
From the yoke
Of a three-dimensional
Reality and I travel
Through the unknown
Headed for a vertical
Column of time.

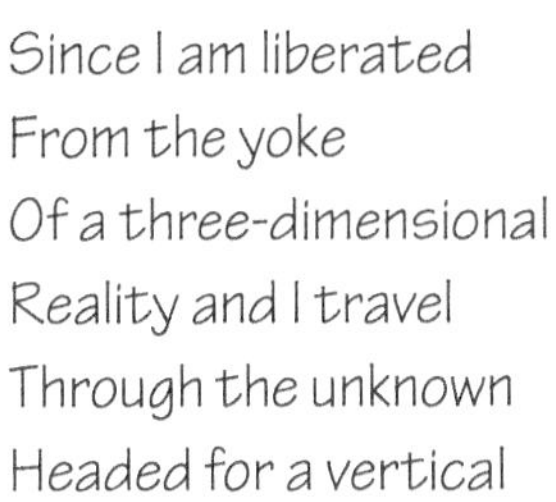

*

As mind expands
Through the unknown
The mystery of life
Defines the doctrine
Of the landscape
And the crystal crow
Takes being toward Truth
To what matters.

Then, the inner eye
Gathers the experiential
Into the launching point
Of Truth, and time and space
Dissolve in the light
Of one-dimensional reality.

As thoughts picture
The connectedness
Of being toward Truth

To the other side
Of time and space
The self joins
The children of promise
In the always already there.

Then, the rhythm of the universe
Releases being there
From constraint and self
Indwells life, liberty
And the pursuit of happiness.

So, being there becomes
Being toward Truth
Through blessed assurance.

So, being there is of the world
While being toward Truth
Is in the world.

*

Passing through the here
And now, gathering Truth
And half-truths mind finds
The contradictions in life
Part of the close at hand
As the absurd becomes
The foundation of what is there

Until the inner eye awakens
To the actual presence
Of The Unknown God.

It is the purpose of the heart
To embrace the presence
Of a vertical column of time
And serve the always already there.

It is the authentic article
Of the way, the Truth
And the life that reaches
Into the outback of mind
As the rhythm
Of the universe speaks
To heart.

Then, the light of The Spirit
Of Wisdom anoints
Being there
With the mystery of life
Being toward Truth
And what matters
Cancels the absurd.

*

It is the passion
Of the crystal crow

That takes thought
Into the mystery of life
As pure music launches
The kiss of the eternal.

It is the deep touch
From the crystal crow
That conveys the light
Of one-dimensional reality
As the rhythm of the universe
Triggers images of the other side
Of time and space.

Although the absurdity
Of the world battles
Against the will to be
The message carried
By the crystal crow
Triumphs, revealing the way
The Truth and the life.

It is the life
In the living moment
That enables a connection
To The Spirit of Wisdom
Through the geometry
Of being toward Truth.

*

In the garden
Of tables and chairs
Where the trumpets of eternity
Announce life, liberty
And the pursuit of happiness
Into the blood of being
Toward Truth
I survey the livi9ng moment
For entrance into the love
Of the way, the Truth
And the life.

There is the message
From the drums of eterni9ty
Pounded into my heart
As the crystal crow
Pyramids The Spirit
Of Wisdom into my third eye
And I picture the unknown.

Then, I drink in the mystery of life.

Then, I climb out of myself
And leap into the wonder
Of the always already there.

So, the living moment
Is there to experience
The love of The Unknown God
As pure music defines

The fearsome symmetry
Of being toward Truth.

*

Then, endless possibility
Opened to eternity
As the mystery of life
Formed images
In the frontier of mind
Triggering wonder
In the here and now.

There were thoughts
That transcended being there
As van awakening
Of the inner eye witnessed
The glory of the house b
Of many mansions
And being toward Truth
Rode the rhythm
Of the universe
Into the always already there.

Then, pure music
From the other side
Of time and space
Reached into my heart
With blessed assurance

And I walked into the light
Of one-dimensional reality.

*

Then, endless possibility
Opened to eternity
As the mystery of life
Formed images
In the frontier of mind
Triggering wonder
In the here and now.

There were thoughts
That transcended being there
As an awakening
Of the inner eye witnessed
The glory of a house
Made of the light
Of one-dimensional reality
And being toward Truth
Followed the rhythm
Of the universe
Into the always already there.

Then, pure music
From the other side
Of time and space
Reached into my heart

With blessed assurance
And I walked into that light
Forevermore.

So, the doctrine
Of the landscape
Is freedom
As I follow my faith
Into the afterlife.

*

SECTION 3:

Sensibility of endless possibility

As the north wind
Penetrates the bone
With cold, the snow
Immaculate in its gown of white
I step into the world
Searching for what matters.

Sitting in the garden
Of tables and chairs
The coffee black and hot
My mind reaches
Into the substance
Of what is there.

In the commerce of being there
Preceding my entrance
The architecture of life
Flaunts its existence
As the community welcomes me
To life, liberty, and the pursuit
Of happiness.

There is a kindness
In the air that generates
A sense of belonging
Although the brutality
Of the north wind
Challenges the living moment.

Wearing the face
Of being toward Truth
My mind nestles
In the arms of the given
Although the war
Of principalities
Rages somewhere else.

I hear the cries
Of the collateral casualties
And smell their burning flesh.

*

It is the chill
Of winter when I harvest
Times and a half
As memories picture
The want of youth.

How the frozen fields
Of snow glisten
With wonder
As I find my place
In the struggle for life
Half here, half there
And the whole
Somewhere else.

Although I stand
Facing the ice storm
I find little choice
But to endure.

To surrender
To the bitter cold
Would be a fate
I cannot accept
As my need for Truth
Feeds into my faith
In The Unknown God.

Looking across the drifts
Of snow that blanket
The here and now
I see my life as a dream
Cast into the winter wind.

*

As the winter wind bites
With snarls and grunts
I feel the call of the crystal crow
With a message from The Spirit
Of Wisdom while pain grips
Each step in the cold.

With one foot
In the grave
And the next step
As excruciating pain
I look for the energy
To carry on.

How life bleeds
From the heart
Of being there.

How visions of death
Seem ever so kind.

Then, I see
The living moment
Fight crippling times
And I take to the cold
With the promise
Of what matters.

There is Truth
In pain that affirms
Life in the living moment
And my friend, my muse
The crystal crow
Lifts each step
To eternity.

*

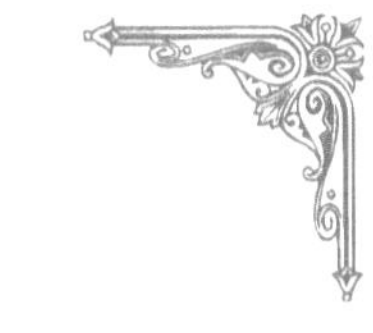

From traces of being there
Trapped in the snow
I look to the north wind
And shiver.

Experiencing life
And playing the hand
I am dealt
I feel the rhythm
Of the universe
With a bankrupt heart.

There is no longer
Time to carve a destiny
On my own
As the hurt cripples
All thought.

As my mind stirs
With the close at hand
And pain paralyzes
My presence
I open my inner eye
To the way, the Truth
And the life
And lean on my faith
Into The Unknown God.

I9t is good to get old
And still have health.

It is sad to get old
And live in pain.

Self-pity is not
A pretty thing.

*

I am never closer
To the love
Of The Unknown God
Than when need drives me
To prayer.

It is in each step
That pain cripples me
And I pray
To the way, the Truth
And the life with every step.

So, it is the need
For mercy that heart
Calls upon help
As a proud man is humbled
By pain learns the grace
Of The Unknown God.

Totally occupying mind
Pain radiates

Through the living moment
As thoughts scatter
Into nothingness.

So, it is when the body
Aches from a walk
Of a few steps
That I pull
Upon my faith for reprieve
And the surgeon's knife
Waits until tomorrow
With healing hands.

So, I feel The Spirit
Of Wisdom teach me
The need for faith.

*

As I enter the other
Side of time and space
I find the place
Of immaculate light
As pure music fills
The living moment
With the will to be.

There is power and strength
In the muscle

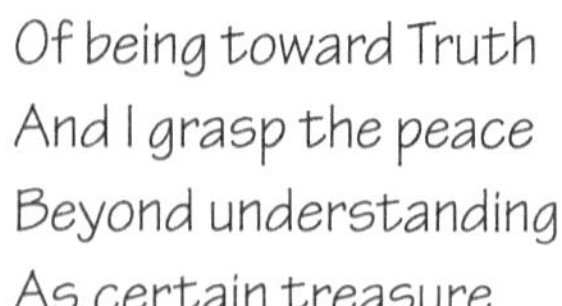

Of being toward Truth
And I grasp the peace
Beyond understanding
As certain treasure.

Then, the crystal crow
Leads me to the origin
Of thought where
The Spirit of Wisdom
Spoke all and everything
Into life.

As a witness to the way
The Truth and the life
I gather the bones
Of eternity
And assemble them
Into an altar
To The Unknown God.

So, I taste life
Liberty and the pursuit
Of happiness
With a thankful heart.

*

Although the winter cold
Freezes the breath of life

The rhythm of the universe
Brings the warmth of pure music
And my mind yearns
For the peace beyond
Understanding.

From the heart of being
Toward Truth echoes
Of the crystal crow
Resonate into purpose
As visions of wonder
Heat the living moment.

So, the powerful energy
Of The Spirit of Wisdom
Allows Truth to form
Thoughts beyond the here
And now as the crystal crow
Celebrates the presence
Of The Unknown God.

Riding the rhythm
Of the universe allows
Mind to travel through
Endless possibility
Far into the reaches
Of the unknown.

Liberating being there
From the darkness yields

Being toward Truth
In the light of the always
Already there
Into the light of the one
Dimensional reality.

So, the continuance
Of being toward Truth
Is my purpose
As I follow the way
The Truth and the life.

*

So, thought takes me
To the other side
Of being there
Where I am kissed with
The dynamic of a vertical
Column of time.

Then, eternity opens
To the quagmire
Of oblivion.

It is the crystal crow
That defends me
From an existential threat
And Truth blossoms
In my heart.

Thinking into endless
Possibility, I gather
Bits of unknown
And follow their shadow
Into the abyss.

Seeing the opaque
Of oblivion
My inner eye
Looks onto the horizon
Of time and space
Searching for what matters

Then, thought connects
To the light of one
Dimensional reality
And I return to my faith
In The Unknown God.

Although through thought
All things are possible
The Truth of The Spirit
Of Wisdom can always
Be trusted.

*

Leaving time and space
Through meditation

And entering the other side
Of being in nothingness
My inner eye takes
Mind into the source
Of thought where the one
Dimensional reality births
Pure music.

There are visions
Of the crystal crow
Dancing across blue waters.

There are parades
Of the children of promise
Honoring the presence
Of The Unknown God.

Then, I read the authentic
Article of the living Truth
From the annals
Of being toward Truth
As the rhythm
Of the universe blankets
Me with loving kindness.

As the mystery of life
Breathes Truth into mind
I return to the here and now
With power, strength
And restored energy.

*

Stepping into the source
Of mind, life
Spins through realities
That do not exist
And I feel the deep touch
That lifts the burden
Of being there.

Then, time present rushes
Onto the other side
Of oblivion, as faith pyramids
Dynamic energy
Into the here and now.

Seeing confusion race
Across time and space
The inner eye pulls
Me into a dance
With being in nothingness.

Then, The Spirit of Wisdom
Delivers me into the actual
And I feel the encompassing
Of Presence reach
From the always already there.

It is that the core
Of being toward Truth

Throbs with the mystery of life
As the crystal crow
Celebrates the way, the Truth
And the life.

*

As the deep touch
Liberates me from the bondage
Of existential being there
I meditate into the light
Of the one-dimensional reality
And endless possibility reveals
The mystery of life.

There is no shadow
To being toward Truth
As my trance reaches
Into a vertical column of time.

Then, the rhythm of the universe
Passes into the unknown.

Then, my inner eye
Pictures the dance
To pure music.

Then, the crystal crow leaps
Into mind with the vision
Of the always already there.

Therefore, I dwell in the authentic
Article of being toward Truth.

*

Penetrating the interstices
Of mind, the rhythm
Of the universe pictures
Pure music and the dance
Of the crystal crow
In the blue of a blue sky.

From the darkness
Of being there, shadows
Of infamy concoct
The abyss
And an existential threat
Burns in the mind.

There is the ache
Of need that writes
Want for relief
Upon time present.

So, I look to the love
Of The Unknown God
For mercy.

As the dawn of faith
Awakens the mind
To being toward Truth
The abyss leaves
Only traces in times
And a half.

So, I reach
For the light of the one
Dimensional reality
As The Spirit of Wisdom
Soothes the agony
Of the here and now.

Then, I dance
With the crystal crow
In the blue of blue skies.

*

How good a cup
Of black coffee
In the morning
As simple pleasures
Feed into the wonder
Of the living moment.

There is the dawn
Of a certain privilege
In seeing the treasures

Of the beyond by dwelling
With a trust
In life, liberty and the pursuit
Of happiness.

It is that being toward Truth
Opens horizons of time
Where the breath
Of the living moment
Carried by the crystal crow
Prospers in the heart.

To live beyond the pain
Of being there
Through meditation
Allows me to build
My dreams into the actual
Manifesting Truth
And not dwelling
In the dread
Of being there.

*

By the light of the full moon
I gather the stones
Leading through the abyss
As echoes of pure music
Dwell in my heart.

To follow Truth
In the midst of chaos
Becomes the purpose
That carries me
Beyond the shadows
Of iniquity.

So, the crystal crow
Basks in the half light
Of the full moon
Waiting for the trumpet
To sound as the world
Sleeps, oblivious of the attack
By being there.

It is that being toward Truth
Is here to preserve and protect
Life, liberty, and the pursuit
Of happiness.

When the full moon flows with
The blood of the children
Of promise, the trumpet sounds
As they give their lives
For the peace
Beyond understanding.

So, I follow
The crystal crow
Into battle
For Truth and justice.

*

The folks in the garden
Of tables and chairs
Know me and I bask
In the warmth of their care.

How the spirit of life
Endures the ache
Of a world gone
Into madness
As the rhythm
Of the universe carries
The heart of kinship
Into times and a half
Soothing the ache
In flesh and blood.

There is a certain comfort
To the compassion
In the garden of tables
And chairs that sings
With pure music
And I am thankful.

As the world explodes
With hatred, the love
From the way, the Truth
And the life makes
More sense.

So, the crystal crow thrives
In the arms of the folks
In the garden of tables
And chairs.

So, you have become
The crystal crow
With the pulse of life
Liberty and the pursuit
Of happiness.

*

During times and a half
When the north wind forbids
Easy travel, the mind centers
On the freshness of the air.

There are promises of spring
But winter steals those thoughts.

Warm in my library
The closeness

Of the always already there
Peals away the illusions
Of being in time
As the inner eye beholds
An awakening to the way
The Truth and the life.

Meditating upon the expanse
The heart feels its way
To what matters as the sun
Lights the dawn of forevermore.

Then, I step to the other side
Of being in nothingness
And eternity brings Truth
To the living moment.

So, I wander through thoughts
Until the crystal crow
Pictures the peace
Beyond understanding.

Then, for the first time
My library makes sense.

SECTION 4

The other in Truth and justice

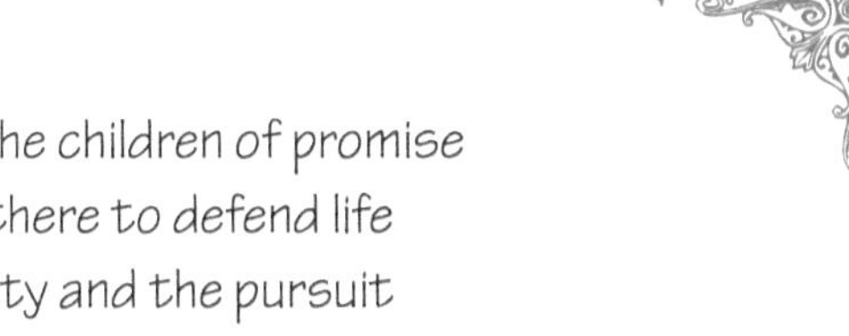

So, the children of promise
Are there to defend life
Liberty and the pursuit
Of happiness
Because all have civil rights.

It is the crystal crow
That connects being toward Truth
To the heart of what matters
As the agony in life leaves
Through times and a half
By following the way
The Truth and the life.

Basking in the light
Of the authentic article
And meditating on
The Spirit of Wisdom
Pictured by pure music
I climb out of self
To witness tho glory
Of The Unknown God.

Then, the drums of eternity
Define the living moment
As a wonder fed
By the rhythm of the universe.

So, the inner eye beholds
The other side of time

And space as a house
Of many mansions in one
Dimensional reality
In a vertical column of time
And populated by the children
Of promise.

*

Triggering thoughts
Of the authentic article
The inner eye pictures
The crystal crow dancing
To the rhythm
Of the universe.

There is the image
Of pure music
Defining the light
Of one-dimensional
Reality as eternity
Colors the living moment
With promise.

As time and space give in
To the victory of being
Toward Truth over being there
The celestial clocks chime
At the hour of forevermore.

Awakening to the crystal crow
I follow the way, the Truth and the life
Into the peace beyond understanding.

Then, the other side
Of the sky pyramids
A clear mind and a pure
Heart into what I
Imagine myself to be
A trumpet
Of The Unknown God.

*

As the sunrises
Over a field of snow
Where bodies are buried
And the garden of tables
And chairs come to life
The living moment pyramids
Time and space into splendor.

To witness the passing
Of the now into the dance
Of the mystery of life
Allows being there to leap
Into being toward Truth
Leaving behind shadows
Of iniquity.

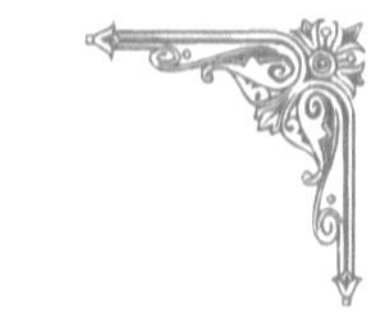

It is with a pure heart
And a clear mind
That being toward Truth
Trumpets the way
The Truth and the life
As being in time
Finds its plot
In the cemetery
Of the no longer.

Then, the philosopher weeps
Over the body of being
And nothingness.

So, the snow glistens
In the presence
Of The Unknown God.

*

The commerce of being there
Focuses upon now points
With little vision of what matters.

The sounds of being there
Are erratic static
Dominating the here and now
As noise is their knowledge.

As time passes
Being there enters oblivion
Yet unaware of its depravity.

To hear the awakening
Of the trumpets of the always
Already there allows Truth
To shine through the light
Of the authentic article
As the way, the Truthy
And the life defines
What matters.

How cumbersome the thoughtless
Province of being there.

*

As the crystal crow
Leaps Into the beyond
Taking me into beauty
And Truth, time and space
Implodes into the light
Of one-dimensional reality.

Through a portal
In the living moment
Mind meditates its way
Into the splendor

Of a vertical column of time
Where pure music delivers
The treasures of the other
Side of being in nothingness.

So, the crystal crow
Carries the message
From The Unknown God
That delivers me
From the darkness
Of being there.

After leaving the here
And now and entering
The presence of the always
Already there, I feel
The pulse of the rhythm
Of the universe.

As I seek a pure heart
And a clear mind
Witnessing the way
The Truth and the life
The mystery of life allows
Me to behold a house
Of many mansions
As my dwelling place
In forevermore

It is the life of the spirit
That endures.

*

As the crystal crow pours
Pure music into the here and now
The children of promise enter
The light of the always
Already there and the shadows
Of being in time fall
Off the edge to oblivion.

It is the beginning
Of forevermore
For the children of promise
As they dance
In the streets of freedom.

So, the spirit continues on
Across the horizon
Of times and a half
As the union
With a vertical column
Of time liberates them
From the dread
Of being in nothingness.

As each individual follows
The way, the Truth
And the life, each receives
The presence of the rhythm
Of the universe
In a dance of eternal joy.

So, the crystal crow
Takes the children of promise
Onto the other side
Of time and space
Through a portal of faith
In The Unknown God.

So, through The Unknown God
All things are possible.

*

So, you are the crystal crow
And your inner eye apprehends
The mystery of life
Through the authentic article.

So, eternity opens
To a house of many mansions
Where pure music celebrates
The living moment of forevermore.

Then, The Spirit of Wisdom kisses
The children of promise
As Truth and beauty dispatch
The crystal crow into time and space.

It is endless possibility
That opens the mind
Allowing you to ride
The rhythm of the universe.

Although being there attempts
To define the way things are
Being toward Truth pyramids
The way, the Truth and the life
From the beyond.

Then, you soar where life begins.

Then you believe your way
Into the splendor
Of The Unknown God.

*

So, you look to the sky
With wonder hoping
To connect to what matters
As clouds cover the beyond.

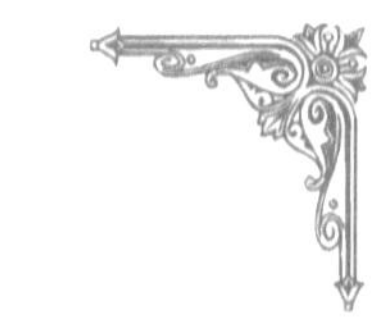

So, purpose and meaning
Hide behind gray masses
And darkness consumes
The living moment.

Then, words jumble
In your mind
In double speak
And philosophers bury you
In senseless rhetoric.

So, what can you
Believe before
Swarming nothingness
And how can you
Trust in the holocaust
Of language?

Then, you feel
The authentic article
Of freedom and time
And space open
To The Spirit of Wisdom.

Then, you feel the faith
Of being toward Truth
And the hope in the way
The Truth and the life.

*

To hear the call
Of the crystal crow
Gladdens your heart
As you eclipse time
And space.

There is the rhythm
Of the universe carrying
You to the living moment
Where the beyond nourishes
You with the promise
Of a pure heart
And a clear mind.

So, the ache of an existential
Threat vanishes as you
Immerse yourself
In the authentic article
As your trust in being
Toward Truth grows.

So, the crystal crow
Is a messenger
From The Spirit of Wisdom
Opening your mind
To the treasures of the beyond.

So, the here and now
Became a steppingstone
To the peace
Beyond understanding.

*

Then, you saw an old man
With his mind set
On a long walk
To eternity, as the days
Were cluttered with struggle.

Stepping across time and space
To a place of an awakening
He composed through his inner eye
An anthem of Truth and beauty,

As he exuded pure music
With his thoughts
Trumpets sounded
And the authentic article
Of being toward Truth
Brought the symmetry
Of splendor.

Then, you watched the old man
Dissolve into the light
Of one-dimensional

Reality, as the crystal crow
Forged The Spirit of Wisdom
In your heart.

So, the old man's life
Became a song following
The rhythm of the universe.

Then, you meditated the way
To the peace beyond understanding.

*

In the garden of tables
And chairs, where thoughts
Penetrate the unknown
An old man stirs
The mystery of life
Into the here and now
As the sun rises over
Fields of glistening snow.

There is stardust in his vision.

Although the bitter bite
Of winter snaps and snarls
Upon being there
Being toward Truth
Reaches into the other side

Of the here and now
To the freshness of life
In the living moment.

Then, the old man feels
The rhythm of the universe
Fill your mind
With the peace
Beyond understanding
As the north wind
Vitalizes your spirit.

Then, the crystal crow
Fills your heart
With The Spirit of Wisdom.

So, experiencing life
And consuming death
Allows access
To the splendor
Of The Unknown God
As you stare upon
The formation
Of pure music
Onto forevermore.

*

It is the will to be
That triumphs, over
The dull round while facing
The chaos of a world
Sold into madness.

It was the greed of some
That jeopardized liberty
In the land of the free and brave.

Then, came the rising
Of individuals, the backbone
Of life, liberty, and the pursuit
Of happiness.

Deep in the heart stirs freedom
And the children of promise
Endowed with being toward Truth
Assemble.

Each has the will to be.

Each has the love of freedom.

So, an old man mans
His post at the edge
Of conflicting agendas.

So, you stare the demigods
In the eye and they crumble

Before the patriots will
For Truth and justice.

*

As the mystery of life
Encompasses the here and now
The actual rises
From freedom of thought
And visions of purpose
And meaning soothes the ache
Of being there.

Where the absurdity
Of being their defiles
The will to be
The crystal crow brings
Truth and justice
Into the living moment.

So, life, liberty, and the pursuit
Of happiness matters.

So, the crystal crow is
A trumpet of The Unknown God
As meditating through
The mystery of life
Onto the peace
Beyond understanding

Carries being toward Truth
Onto the authentic article
Of beauty and wonder.

Then, thoughts of the mystery
Of life liberates mind
From the constraints
Of the dull round
And the crystal crow eases
A message of faith, hope
And love across horizons
Of time.

*

As the celestial clocks
Wind down to the hour
That ends time and space
I look into the darkness
And weep.

Then, a beam of light
Spearheads the here and now
Brought by the crystal crow
And the message blossoms
With hope.

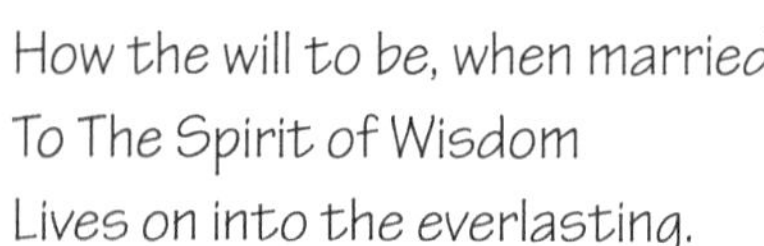

How the will to be, when married
To The Spirit of Wisdom
Lives on into the everlasting.

Although it was a nightmare
When devils inflicted pain
Smashing the here and now
It became the living moment
Filled with love from The
Unknown God that endured.

So, the way the Truth
And the life triggered hope
In the heart of being
Toward Truth.

So, the rhythm of the universe
Carries life onto forevermore
Preserving and protecting
The children of promise.

*

To fight the pain
To endure devastation
How the will to be
Overcomes the affliction.

Although the ache is deep
The Spirit of Wisdom

Infuses the strength
To carry on, as each step
Is filled with the love
Of The Unknown God.

So, the authentic article
Of the way, the Truth
And the life endows
The will to be with the power
To conquer the infirmity.

Struggling through the disability
Allows you to hear
The crystal crow pronounces
What matters, as the here
And now collapses in agony.

Then, you feel pure music
Strengthen your bone and muscle
As you ride the rhythm
Of the universe.

So, the message
From the crystal crow
Frees you from debilitation
As your will to be
Stands tall in power and strength.

*

Listening to the call
Of the crystal crow
You trumpet times
And a half into being
Toward Truth.

The message generates
Passage into life, liberty
And the pursuit of happiness.

It is the strength
Born by faith
In The Unknown God
That allows you
To overcome adversity.

It is the power
Of The Spirit of Wisdom
That grants you
A clear mind and a pure heart
The necessities for probing
The unknown.

So, the call of the crystal
Crow infuses a right spirit
Upon you through the way
The Truth and the life
As the actual presents
Itself as what matters.

Although there are
Many realities for being there
There is only one
Actuality born from the one
Dimensional reality
And given to being toward
Truth, only.

*

As pure music surrounds
Being toward Truth
With the mystery of life
The inner eye beholds
The other side of the here
And now.

It is the coming and going
Of time present
That magnifies the need
For purpose and meaning
As the living moment feeds
Being toward Truth
With the authentic article.

As the living moment
Expands across time and space
The horizon of what matters
Emerges.

It is the dwelling
In the living moment
That allows being
Toward Truth
To transcend the world
Gone into madness.

So, being toward Truth
Purposes itself
Into pure music
By riding the rhythm
Of the universe
To behold the other
Side if the here and now.

So, the here and now
Becomes only the shadow
Of the living moment.

To dwell in the living moment
Allows you access
To the mystery of life.

*

Looking through the looking
Glass of the mystery of life
You gather the deep touch
Of what matters

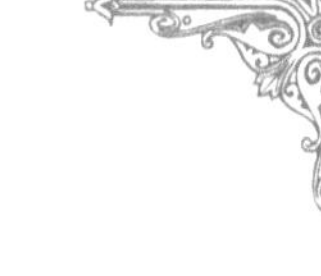

As the world descends
Into being in nothingness.

The existential threat
That hammers your brain
Does not ease up
Until you feel pure
Music from beyond.

There is a peace
Beyond understanding
That accompanies
Meditating upon The Spirit
Of Wisdom
And the ache in life
Leaves from the shadows
Beneath mind.

Then, you see
The library of concepts
With books of purpose
And meaning.

Then, you will write
Your name in the stars
As the celestial clocks carry
You onto the authentic
Article of being toward Truth.

*

It is the blood shed
From the crystal crow
That instill the elixir
Of the living moment
With the mystery
Of life as the pursuit
Of Truth takes you
To the presence
Of life and liberty.

As the trumpet of the always
Already sounds freedom
Into the heart of being toward
Truth, the stars read the passage
Of time and space into you.

Then, the deep touch
Takes your mind
Into visions of the other
Side of the here and now.

Then, The Spirit of Wisdom
Speaks the authentic article
Of being toward Truth
Into the encompassing
And you know the way
The Truth and the life.

As time and times
And a half pass through the eyes
Of the crystal crow you learn
To trust The Unknown God.

So, Truth liberates
Who you are
From the here and now.

*

To gain a pure heart
And a true mind
Learn to trust the way
The Truth and the life
Written by the hand
Of The Spirit of Wisdom.

There is hope through
The love of The Unknown God.

It is that the center
Of the mystery of life
Is the one-dimensional
Reality and the light
Of the always already there.

It is the encompassing
Of a vertical column of time

That is your destiny
As your faith carries you
To a house of many mansions.

As your mind awakens
To Truth, the rhythm
Of the universe takes
You into the peace beyond
Understanding and shadows
Of thought fade into the void.

So, the Truth sets you free
From the choking entanglements
Of a world sold into madness.

*

As the bite of nothingness
Snaps in your face
The mind cringes and worlds
Charge into madness.

There is the echo
Of Truth filtering
Through the debris
Scattered acr5oss time
And space.

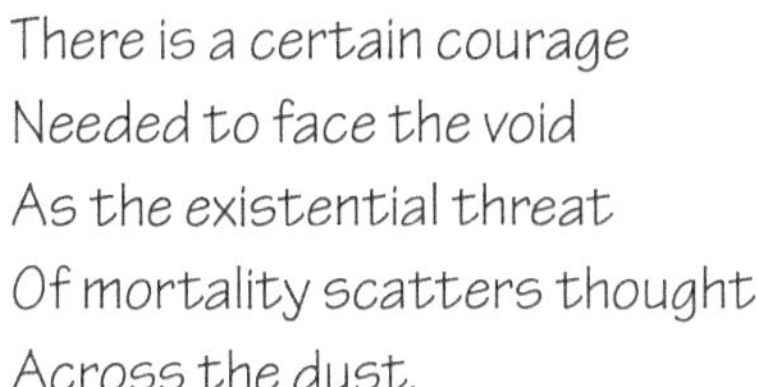

There is a certain courage
Needed to face the void
As the existential threat
Of mortality scatters thought
Across the dust.

As a young man I saw
Death as something that happens
To others but now
I see its look piercing my brain.

So, it is part
Of the mystery of life
Lurking behind the scene
Until its immanence
Before time present.

Then, I feel the love
Of The Unknown God
As hope leads to understanding
Filling the void with peace
And death has no dominion.

*

Although the crystal crow
Exists as an idea
Residing in the beyond
It brings passion

Into the heart
And liberty in the mind
For the living moment.

As the here and now
Dissolves in a blur
And madness collapses the world
The crystal crow fortifies
Being toward Truthy
With the strength to endure.

So, there are those
Who are the oppressors
And those oppressed.

While the oppressor's feed
Upon their will to power
The oppressed only
Desire to live and let live.

Then, here is war
Because Lady Liberty has
A will for freedom.

So, the crystal crow weeps
Over the carnage of war.

*

From the depths
Of the deep touch
The crystal crow launches
A message from The Spirit
Of Wisdom.

Liberating the living moment
From the madness of the world
You meditate your way
To pure music
As your heart seeks
The rhythm of the universe.

Then, visions take
Your mind into the geometry
Of being toward Truth.

It is an awakening
To what matters
As you drink in
The authentic article
And you feel the crystal
Crow's message.

How your thoughts grow
Into the encompassing
Of the one-dimensional
Reality as you breathe
The breath of eternity.

Then, you behold the way
The Truth and the life.

So, you learn to trust
The Unknown God.

*

So, two old men
Walk down the hill
One black, one white.

They share the same vision
As time only strengthens
Their friendship.

Although the world spins
Hatred across the land
They listen to the rhythm
Of the universe together
As pure music opens
Their hearts to eternity.

It is the bond of men
That punctuates life
With the breath
Of freedom as two old
Men advance in time
Together.

Since they see
The same sunrise
And follow the same dance
Of the moon
Their lives walk in peace
As equals before the always
Already there.

So, two old men speak
The language of peace
Through their walk
Down the hill, together.

*

Vanishing in the debris
Of a world sold
Into madness, I feel the void
That cancels life, liberty
And the pursuit of happiness
As the wind carries
My thoughts from the beyond.

It is the echo of Truth
That you find in my absence
And the crystal crow
Becomes my companion
In the center of nothingness.

Then, we meditate our way
Into the living moment
And we appear
As visions of forevermore.

It is our connection
To The Unknown God
That returns us
To the land of the free
And the brave
Through the rhythm
Of the universe.

Then, the crystal crow
Speaks the language
Of The Spirit of Wisdom
And I climb out of myself
Into the presence of the way
The Truth and the life.

So, we give thanks
At the altar of the King of kings
The Unknown God.

*

Looking eye to eye
With the crystal crow
You gather the beauty

Of pure music that emanates
From the other side
Of time and space
As the look of winter
Spawns the authentic
Article.

Although you feel
The intensity in the contact
There is a subtle peace
Through the looking glass
The eyes of the crystal crow.

Then, the crystal crow
Takes you into the deep touch
Of the rhythm of the universe
And your heart beats
With passion for life.

It is the vibration
In waves from pure music
That defines the living moment
As you trust The Spirit of Wisdom.

So, you feel the presence
Of The Unknown God
Anointing you
With blessed assurance.

*

Meditating on the authentic
Article with thoughts
Riding on the rhythm
Of the universe, you see
The substance of what matters
And pure music fills
Your heart with life.

To envision the meat
Of being toward Truth
Allows the spirit
To manifest endless
Possibility, as time
Configures the passage
Of the here and now
Into the living moment.

Then Truth empowers
The strength to endure.

Then, purpose flows
Through the stars
As the celestial clocks
Chime the lives
Of the children of peace
Into a destiny of glory.

So, there is freedom
In the presence
Of The Unknown God.

Although the world is
Filled with darkness, the light
Of Truth lives on.

*

As pure music awakens
Being toward Truth
To the star dust
Of forevermore
Mind navigates
Through the unknown
To the other side
Of existential threats.

As the drums of eternity
Cast the light of one
Dimensional reality
Into the living moment
Heart follows the rhythm
On the universe into the always
already there.

Then, the authentic article
Of blessed assurance

Issues the purpose
Of blood, bone and brain
And you gather
The substance of what matters
As the domain of Truth.

So, the crystal crow guides you
With the message
From The Spirit of Wisdom.

Then, you breathe in pure music.

*

SECTION 5

The ache of absurdity

After sleeping a restful night
I awoke to blood on my doorstep.

Across the globe
Flags of freedom lowered
To half-mast as a critical
Evil reared its ugly head.

It was the sound
Of bombs bursting
Rocking the graveyards
Of freedom's patriots
And the mind of the world
Revolted against the tyrant.

More blood shall be shed.

It is that the life of freedom
Comes at a cost
To fight the good fight
For life, liberty and the pursuit
Of happiness.

Beware tyrants: Lady Liberty
Is a mighty force.

So, The Spirit of Wisdom
Writes the tyrant's name
In the Book of Shame
As he vomits his death.

*

Then, it became the time
When the crystal crow
Dissolved the language
Of the here and now
And all of space turned
To blood.

Then, the drums
Of eternity pounded
The rhythm of the universe
Into the physics
Of time and space
And the living moment
Altered the structure
Of knowledge.

Darkness filled the days
With silence and the tongues
Of being there turned to rust.

So, the trumpet sounded
Pure music of forevermore
And the sky disappeared.

It was a time of upheaval.

So, the trumpet sounded mercy
Upon the children of promise

As their lives were spared
From annihilation.

Then, the children of promise
Walked in peace
Thriving in what matters.

*

As tears roll down
Hour after hour
I move the silence in my mind
Into platitudes
While trying to get a grip.

There was the pounding
Of my heart into bloody meat
That lifted my eyes
Into the unknown.

How the time aches.

So, the madness in the world
Battles against hope
That wanted a living moment of peace.

Then, the crystal crow
Speaks Truth into the present
And you bury life with the dead.

How, ruthless men
Design a world
Of madness, but you
And the crystal crow
Form the living moment
Into the peace beyond understanding
Through The Spirit of Wisdom.

*

Although the struggle is
Great, the will of being
Toward Truth faces the challenge
With courage and determination.

Although bombs burst over head
Being toward Truth
Combats the enemy
With a passion for freedom.

There is no threat great
Enough to cripple
The will of being toward Truth.

In the belly of the enemy
Is softness
As its constitution
Whimpers in shadows.

Daggers of patriots strike
The heart of an enemy
That flaunts its foolishness.

So, Lady Liberty reconstitutes
The power of freedom
Into a force, indeed, formidable.

So, the world unites
And rockets support
The free and the brave.

Hell has no wrath
Then when Lady Liberty
Is spurned.

So, the will of being
Toward Truth endures.

*

In the valley of all
Time and space
The rhythm of the universe
Awakens primordial mind
To the authentic article.

It is a beckoning
From the crystal crow

That musters being
Toward Truth to the front lines
Of existential threats.

As being in nothingness
Encircles what is there
The children of promise
Focus their substance
On the way, the Truth
And the life.

Then, the earth of being there
Crumbles into waste
As their minds rust
And the drums of eternity
Pound deliverance for the children
Of promise into the peace
Beyond understanding.

It is by the hand
Of The Unknown God
That tyrants consume
Their own blood as the world
Turns to freedom.

*

Riding the rhythm
Of the universe, you

Reach into a pocket
Of stars to feel
The presence in the always
Already there.

It is that the world dissolves
In a sea of blood
As war devours liberty.

Then, Lady Liberty charges
The tyrants with the fury
Of the steadfast
And time bleeds into the lives
Of what matters.

It was a testament
To freedom that touched
The heart of the world
As you faced the tyrants
With courage and determination.

So, the tyrants consumed
Themselves
Amid the devastation
Of their own making.

Although the tyrants
Attacked the lands
Of freedom, you tore out
The heart of their nations

While riding the rhythm
Of the universe.

*

In the library of the peace
Beyond understanding
The books of life, liberty
And the pursuit of happiness
Dance to the rhythm
Of the universe.

There is a beauty
To live with Truth
As life embraces life
With the fervor
Of the deep touch.

So, time enters one
Dimensional reality
In this library
As you channel The Spirit
Of Wisdom.

So, the greatest things
That The Unknown God
Created are the heavens
And the earth
One universe governed

By the way, The Truth
And the life.

Then, you ride
The rhythm of the universe
Into the always already there
As the dawn of time
And times and a half
Emerge with glory.

It is the cold
Juxtaposition of messages
Yielding to warm
Connectivity that defines
The books in this library.

*

As time and space collapse
The light of one
Dimensional reality encompasses
The void of being there.

While the sediments
Of nothingness explode
Into volumes of works
Being toward Truth faces
The tyrants over the here
And now that starve the world
Into submission.

The cries of the masses
Deafening as they are
Fuel the fire
That consumes them.

So, The Unknown God
Living as a vertical
Column of time embraces
The children of promise
With hope and the anatomy
Of being their plunges
Into darkness.

Then, time and space
Becomes the graveyard
Of yesterday, the stirring
Of Truth into mind.

Although Truth is immortal
The existence of being there
Suffers forevermore.

To exist in hell forevermore
A grievous state of affairs.

*

As time and space collapse
The light of one

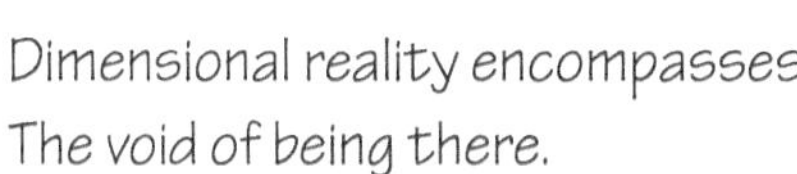

Dimensional reality encompasses
The void of being there.

While the sediments
Of nothingness explode
Into volumes of works
Being toward Truth faces
The tyrants over the here
And now that starve the world
Into submission.

Although the cries of the people
Deafening as they are
Do not save them
From the fire that consumes them.

As The Unknown God
Lives as a vertical column
Of time embraces the children
Of promise with hope
The anatomy of being
There plunges into darkness.

Then, time and space
Become the graveyard
Of yesterday, the stirring
Of Truth into mind.

Although Truth endures
Forevermore

The existence of being there
Suffers forevermore.

*

Meditating with the deep touch
I see Truth in the living moment
As time and times and a half
Explode into star dust.

Slipping into a two
Dimensional reality, I picture
The face of what matters
And an anthem of hope
Triumphs over the madness
Of the world.

Then The Spirit of Wisdom
Punctuates being toward Truth
And I eclipse time and space
As pure music defines
The living moment.

So, you climb out of yourself
And witness the vertical
Column of time.

So, you pass through
The unknown as your mind

Reaches into the living moment
And a trumpet signals,
The beginning of another era.

Then the authentic
Article lifts visions
Of what matters
Across being toward Truth.

*

Delving into the unknown
While equipped with the power
Of the deep touch
You possibility as the oppressors
Cry for mercy.

To deliver the message
Of freedom across the globe
The crystal crow launches
The will to be
Into your heart
As being toward Truth
Neutralizes the oppressors.

The tyrants dissolve into nothingness
And you bury them
In caverns of the forgotten.

Then, the world leaves
Its madness
As your inner eye
Envisions what matters.

It is that you side
With the strength
Of Lady Liberty
As the always already
There shows you
The endless possibility
Of The Unknown God.

*

There is in the chambers
Of your heart the passion
For pure music carrying
Thoughts of Truth in true beauty.

As the melody of time
And space trace meaning
Into your mind, you
Grow into the destiny
Written in the stars.

It is the embodiment of Truth
That liberates the doctrine
Of the landscape while

The Spirit of Wisdom
Infuses the authentic
Article in your mind.

Then, a small land
Rebukes a large invader
And the drums of eternity
Carry freedom across the world.

So, the life of freedom
Sacrifices the blood
Of the children of promise
As the invaders collapse
In their loss.

Although the cost of freedom
Is great, there is no other way
To live with dignity.

*

To incite the minds
To the mystery of life
Pure music signals
An abundance of thought
And the meaning of the message
Awakens being there
To being toward Truth.

It is the rhetoric
Of some times
That dismisses Truth
But the crystal crow
Announces the anthem
Of hope.

As The Unknown God
Dawns the way, the Truth
And the life, you stand
At the threshold
Of an awesome wonder
And the signature of what
Matters signs access
To the other side
Of being in nothingness.

So, you follow the drift
Of pure music releasing
The minds of the world
Into the always already
There.

Then, you rise
Into radiant splendor
Climbing out of yourself.

*

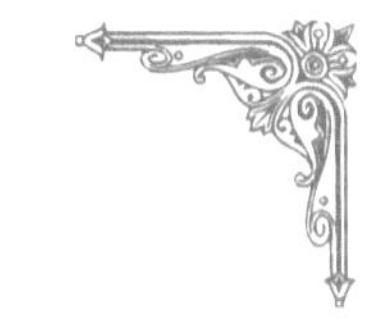

As words dissolve
Into pure music
You feel the voice
Of times and a half
And the signature
Of what matters writes
Across your heart
With the deep touch.

Then, the crystal crow takes
You into one-dimensional reality.

Then, The Spirit of Wisdom
Trumpets being toward
Truth alongside The Unknown God.

It is the mystery
Of life that brings you
Into the other side
Of being in time
As being there, crumbles
Beneath its own weight.

Then, star dust fills
Your heart with hope
And the living moment
Explodes the here and now
Into your mind with the face
Of the always already there.

*

So, there are only
Three dimensions
But multiple realities
And you travel
To the other side
Of time and space
By riding the rhythm
Of the universe.

It is the pure music that inhabits
The source of the living moment
Birthed by The Spirit of Wisdom
That moves you into star dust.

Then, all of matter is the wall
Between imagination and reason
Constructing time with now points
A theoretical concept.

Although the intersection
Of time past and time future
Founds time present
It is only a theory
Because life dwells
In the living moment
And that is what matters.

It is a time binding of The Unknown God
Registered in being toward Truth
That allows mankind of life.

Then, The Architect of all
And everything builds
Truth within your heart.

*

Awakening to the dawn
That brings enlightenment
You envision the face
Of what matters
And time and space exOplode
Into the living moment.

It is when pure music
Takes your heart
Into loving kindness
And the way, the Truth
And the life walks with you
Onto forevermore.

So, the drums of eternity
Move your mind
Into the peace beyond
Understanding and the living
Moment fulfills your destiny.

Then, the war of principalities ends.

Then, your heart is pure
And your mind is clear.

Although tribulation is
A part of life
The Spirit of Wisdom
Sees you through the chaos.

So, you walk tall
With the presence
Of The Unknown God.

*

Then, you saw the man
Made of bricks
As his blood flowed
Over the indwelling
Of time and space.

Although being there disappears
In the thick of time
Being toward Truthy advances
Across the globe.

Although the world rejects
Domination by the tyrants

The struggle for freedom
And individual dignity
Carries on.

Then, Lady Liberty takes
You to the heart
Of the mystery of life
And you behold
The destiny of mankind.

Thundering through the streets
The crystal crow proclaims
Pure music across times
And your inner eye
Rides the rhythm
Of the universe onto the peace
Beyond understanding.

So, the man of bricks
Builds your life into a fortress
Of Truth and beauty.

*

There is a voice
Among the multitude
That trumpets the authentic
Article into the blood
Of what matters.

It is a voice
Of pure music
Carried by the wind
And it liberates minds
From the despair
Of lives lost
In the madness
Of a convoluted world.

To see Truth
Through the looking glass
Of the mystery of life
You gather strength
And you endure aa being
Toward Truth.

Then, you shun nothingness.

Then, you feel the rhythm
Of the universe
Unfold in splendor.

So, the voice of the mystery
Of life sings the will
To be into the multitude
Establishing freedom
As a way of life for all.

*

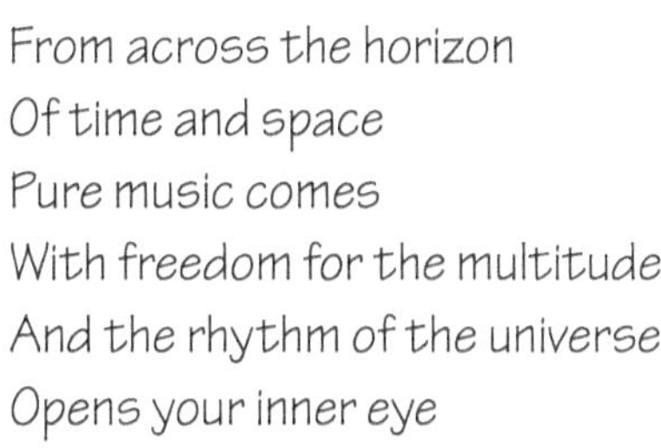

From across the horizon
Of time and space
Pure music comes
With freedom for the multitude
And the rhythm of the universe
Opens your inner eye
To the authentic article.

Basking in the true light of one
Dimensional reality, your mind
Actualizes the living moment
To reveal the mystery of life.

Although infamy hides
In shadows, you know
The madness of its intent.

Although shadows desire
To silence Lady Liberty
The gravity of the celestial
Clocks speaks the will to be
Into the multitude.

You will not give in to the tyrants.

As times and a half
Uncover Truth, you rise
In the living moment to break
The oppressor's hold.

*

As the drama of the world's
Madness chokes time present
Being toward Truth
Trumpets The Spirit
Of Wisdom into the hearts
And minds of the multitude.

Although chaos abounds
The Unknown God
Offers the way, the Truth
And the life as mana
Feeding being toward Truth
With the will to be.

How demons dance
Over their own demise.

So, a land of liberty
Faces these demons
With victory in its heart.

It is the war of principalities
That targets the children
Of promise, as Lady Liberty
Fearless, takes her stand.

So, you gather strength
In your bones, as your

Muscles pump determination
Into your fight
With the blood thirsty.

*

As the world aches
For peace, the crystal
Crow delivers a message
From The Spirit of Wisdom
But the madness in the world
Does not listen.

It is that the children
Cry out for deliverance4
While politicians, posture
Empty rhetoric
Doing too little too late.

So, the children of promise
Take on the Invaders
While bombs rip
Into the lives of those
Who want to live
In freedom.

It is the will to power
That flaunts its folly
As it attacks the foundation
Of civilization.

How echoes of suffering
Rise across the ashes.

Then, the crystal crow
Takes the hand of Lady
Liberty and together they triumph
Over the madness
Of the power mongers.

*

It is a calling
From The Spirit of Wisdom
That reaches into your heart
As your mind wills you to endure.

To conquer your suffering
The crystal crow writes
The hope for the peace
Beyond understanding
Across the sunrise.

Although the flame of passion
Flickers in the wind
It lights the world
To the blessing of freedom.

Facing the darkness
Of oppression

The children of promise
Arm themselves with the way
The Truth and the life
As the tyrants consume
Their own blood.

Then, the trumpet sounds
Across the earth
Lifting your heart
To the splendor
Of what truly matters.

It is The Unknown God
That has delivered you.

*

As the missals of terror
Destroy the lives of cities
In a land where children
Of promise once prospered
In liberty, you look at war
As the history of mankind.

How the power mongers
Drink the blood
Of one nation after another.

Life is worthless
Or so the tyrants think.

They have no heart
No soul, as they explode
The substance of mankind.

Then, comes The Spirit
Of Wisdom swallowing
The madness and time
Cancels the muscle
Of the oppressors.

So, Lady Liberty flourishes
In the dawn of the way
The Truth and the life.

Soon comes the time
When the accounts
Of the power mongers
Are settled and they will
Pay for inflicting suffering.

*

When the struggle for life
Exceeds the will to be
There remains hope to conquer
The adversity, the ache.

So, you cry out for mercy
But silence abounds.

Then, you turn
To the love of the way
The Truth and the life.

In the heart of being
Toward Truth
The rhythm of the universe
Connects to your will to be
Fueling you with the power
To endure.

As one painful step
After another encroaches
Upon you, you feel the love
Of The Unknown God
And the compassion
Of pure music.

So, from the other side
Of time and space, you
Gather the fortitude
To endure.

*

There is death in the wind
The death of a tyrant
And the celestial clocks
Strike the hour of his demise.

How a multitude suffered
Under his command
But the children of promise
Rise to the light of freedom.

So, the will to be
Through The Spirit
Of Wisdom triumphs
Over the will to power
As a snake is slain
In chambers of blood.

As being toward Truth
Waves the flag of liberty
The multitude is released
From their chains.

Conquering over evil
The will to be liberates
Control over hearts
And minds of people
As the multitude tastes
The bread and wine
Of the way, the Truth
And the life.

So, Lady Liberty prays
To The Unknown God.

*

Because there is war
And there are always wars
The people suffer
As the power mongers
Dine on the flesh of freedom.

Dissecting the heart
Of liberty lovers
The world arms the oppressors
And a multitude is murdered.

There can be no peace
In the world
As long as there are those
Who slaughters the children
Of promise for the sake
Of those who hunger for power.

As the drums of eternity
Pound freedom into the heart
Of the people
The oppressors burn
In their own ashes.

To persevere, Lady Liberty
Waves her birth right
And the man of bricks
Fortifies a resistance
Against the tyrants.

Then, you feel the power
Of universal human rights.

SECTION 6

Purposing pure music

Connecting to the crystal crow
Allows you to envision the elements
Of time onto space
As pure music takes you
Into the authentic article.

Then, the unknown eases
Into the living moment
As the looking glass
Of the mystery of life
Shines through your inner eye.

When time and times and a half
Crumble in the twilight
The dawn of being toward Truth
Comes from the other side
Of the absurd and trumpets alert
Time present in the living moment.

Then, the crystal crow
Connects you to natural elements
And the earth of pure music
Moves you from shadows
Into the light of the one
Dimensional reality.

So, predestination is only
Viewed from a vertical
Column of time.

*

As time collides with space
And the trumpet sounds
The world collapses
In a nightmare of absurdity.

There is a tremor
Of words that takes you
Into the mystery of life
While the unknown fills
Your heart with the juice
Of the living moment.

Then, you behold the authentic
Article while the ghost
Of being there haunts
Your thoughts.

Then, the presence
Of being toward Truth
Eclipses the chaos.

Beholding Truth as it is
Tears down the walls
That separate you
From what matters
As time onto space breathes
In The Spirit of Wisdom.

*

Leaving behind absurdity
I climb outside of myself
And breathe in The Spirit
Of Wisdom as the light
Of one-dimensional reality
Opens my inner eye
To life, liberty and the pursuit
Of happiness.

Calling across time onto space
The crystal crow pronounces the way
The Truth and the life
To the children of promise.

As the living moment takes
Me into a parabola of time
You witness the crystal crow echo
The rhythm of the universe
And your tongue learns
The language of Truth.

Then, the drums of eternity
Pound the love of The Unknown
God into your heart.

*

Easing into the unknown
As the crystal crow connects
You to The Spirit of Wisdom
You feel the rhythm
Of the universe bring breath
To being toward Truth
And the trumpet of the always
Already there awakens
The mystery of life
In your brain.

There is the light
Of one-dimensional
Reality taking you
To time onto space
And you read the language
Of the everlasting in the wind.

Suddenly, the sky opens
To a house of many mansions.

Then you feel what matters.

Then, the crystal crow
Signals the entrance of the way
The Truth and the life.

*

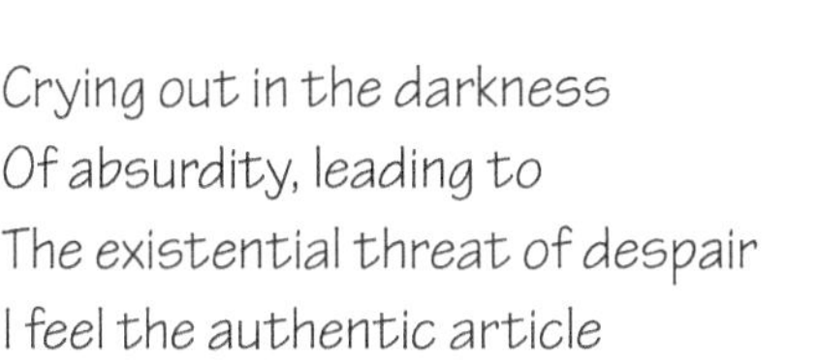

Crying out in the darkness
Of absurdity, leading to
The existential threat of despair
I feel the authentic article
Known by those who suffer.

It is that the ghost
Of being there haunts
The living moment
With terror.

As time becomes the blood
Of life to space
I breathe in The Spirit
Of Wisdom, while the rhythm
Of the universe carries you
Into the peace beyond
Understanding.

Then, your mind bends
To gusts of thought
While you crawl out
Of yourself.

So, you and I carried
The weight of absence.

Then, the anthem of hope
Comes from the way
The Truth and the life.

*

Crawling out of despair
While the absurd haunted
Time present, I felt
The rhythm of the universe
Caress my cheek
With loving kindness
As the madness of the world
Covered me with darkness.

It was the will to endure
Infused by The Spirit of Wisdom
That took time onto space
Into my heart and death
Had no dominion.

It was the search for Truth
That took you from the depths
Of despair.

It was your desire for meaning
In a meaningless world that opened
Your inner eye to the light
Of one-dimensional reality.

So, you learned the tongue
Of the way, the Truth and the life.

Then, you felt the seed
Of being toward Truth grow
In the garden of plenty.

*

To suffer the agony
Of being there. I had
Known pain
As the world spun
In absurdity
In a pool of blood.

It was a reckless ride
Across time and space
That drove me into defeat
As the sky filled
With the blood of tears.

So, the times crushed me
And crippled, I cried out
In the silence of despair.

So, I picked up my bones
And headed to relief
Through my will to be.

How the struggle through pain
Pictured the authentic article
Of being toward Truth.

It was faith in deliverance
Through the way, the Truth
And the life that opened
My mind to what mattered.

As I suffered, I saw
The other side of agony
And continued on with hope.

*

Riding the rhythm
Of the universe you
Become star dust in the everlasting
As the mystery of life
Shows the teeth of the unknown
Grind time onto space
Into bloody meat.

There is violence in the air.

As the earth of being there
Crumbles, you look beyond devastation
And the absurdity of destruction.

Then, the crystal crow brings
You the mana of life
Liberty and the pursuit
Of happiness.

Then being toward Truth
Breathes freedom in the living
Moment as Lady Liberty emanates
Pure music surrounding your space.

It is the rhythm of the universe
That carries life into your heart
As your mind grows with what matters.

As the authentic article
Equips you with the will
To be, the peace
Beyond understanding indwells
The elements of your space.

*

Meditating upon the light
Of one-dimensional reality, you
Advance into a parabola of time
Where splendor poses in your mind.

The image that is there
Becomes a testament
To the authentic article
Giving birth
To what matters.

As the sky opens
To the mystery of life

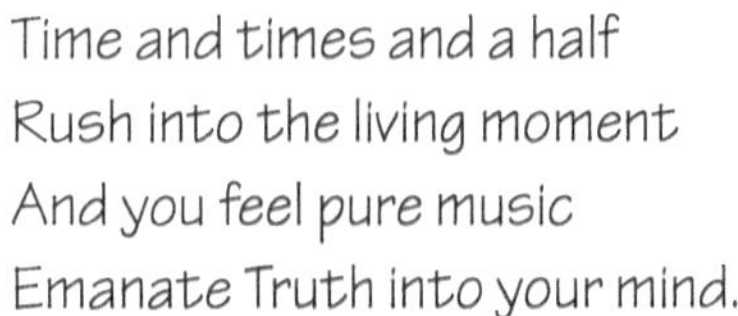

Time and times and a half
Rush into the living moment
And you feel pure music
Emanate Truth into your mind.

It is passage into the always
Already there through the inner eye.

It is the element
Of the peace beyond
Understanding.

Then, your heart feels
The rhythm of the universe
As a two-dimensional reality
Pictures life, liberty
And the pursuit of happiness.

It is the light of one
Dimensional reality
That teaches the way,
The Truth and the life.

*

As time rushed me
Into the absurdity
Of being there, space
Consumed the living moment
Through your inner eye.

There was only the call
Of the crystal crow
From beyond the here and now
Until being toward Truth
Harnessed the treasures
Of the mystery of life.

Although you were given a pure heart
And a clear mind, it was only
The beginning of a long journey
Into the unknown.

It was time onto space
That divided time
From times and a half
As the celestial clocks
Struck purpose
Into the living moment.

Because you sensed
The deep touch
Of a vertical column
Of time, your journey
Took you to the other
Side of absurdity.

So, your life began again.

*

It is that the crystal crow
Speaks the language
Of the mystery of life
And the earth trembles.

Probing the secrets
Of being in time
The crystal crow launches
Meaning from times
And a half as the wind
Blows Truth
Onto the landscape.

It is the will to power
That nullifies the will
To be.

Then, the mind rejects
The oppressors
Molding what matters
From shadows of silence
The unknown.

So, you listen to the call
Of the crystal crow
Your muse as the rhythm
Of the universe
Takes you into folds
Of pure music.

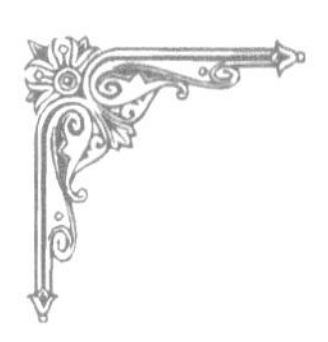

Although the celestial clocks
Hold the secrets of the universe
You visit Truth upon wings
Of the crystal crow.

*

Breathing in the light
Of one-dimensional
Reality, you travel
Through the unknown
And feel the *deep* touch
Of the always already there.

Although silence has ruled
For more than times
And a half, pure music
Breaks through the void
As you trumpet being
Toward Truth.

Then, in the garden
Of tables and chairs
The crystal crow weighs
The substance of what
Matters and you read Truth
From the script
Of cosmic consciousness.

As you meditate
On the rhythm
Of the universe, the mystery
Of life forms an image
Of the everlasting
And the will to power
Ignores its folly.

So, you envision the other
Side of time onto space.

Then, the other side
Of time onto space
Is the dwelling of one
Dimensional reality.

*

Here in the garden
Of tables and chairs
The crystal crow speaks
The language of the everlasting
And time onto space
Infuses life through The Spirit
Of Wisdom.

It is the mystery of life
That shoulders the unknown
As the4 secrets of the always
Already there appear

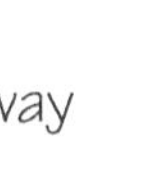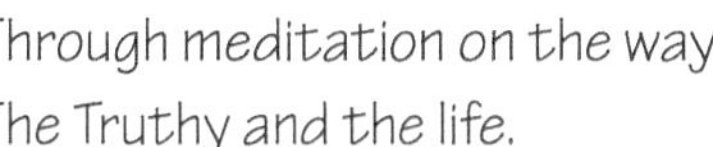

Through meditation on the way
The Truthy and the life.

Listening to pure music
Carried by the wind
You gather what matters
From the madness
Of the world until Truth
Opens your mind
To a vertical column of time.

Then, the crystal crow
Your muse takes
You onto the other side
Of the here and now
Where the living moment
Prospers.

As your heart leaps
Into the stars, you feel
The rhythm of the universe
And The Unknown God smiles.

It is The Unknown God
That liberates you
From the madness
Of the world.

*

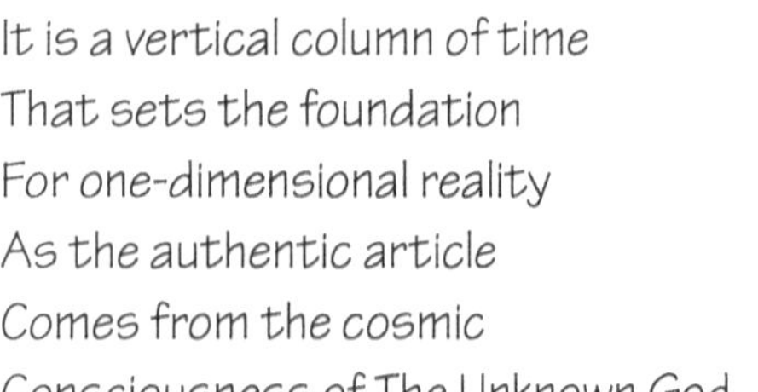

It is a vertical column of time
That sets the foundation
For one-dimensional reality
As the authentic article
Comes from the cosmic
Consciousness of The Unknown God.

So, the entire domain
Of ideas comes
From the deep touch
Of the rhythm of the universe
The breath of The Spirit
Of Wisdom.

Through meditation being
Toward Truth reaches
Into cosmic consciousness
As the will to be grows
Into pure music.

So, you gather thoughts
Of what matters
As the freedom of being
Toward Truth follows
The way, the Truth
And the life.

So, your thoughts form
As supplements to the deep
Touch of the always

Already there, the presence
Of The Unknown God.

*

As the will to be
Gathers the strength to endure
The pains in life subside
And the sky opens to promise.

There is the time to take in
The splendor of what
Is there as the sky
Glistens with radiant majesty.

Then, from the other side
Of the universe, the crystal
Crow calls pure music to fill
Your mind with treasures
And your heart takes
To the rhythm of the universe.

It is through meditating
Upon the beauty of creation
That conquers the ills
In the madness of the world.

Following time and times
And a half to the everlasting

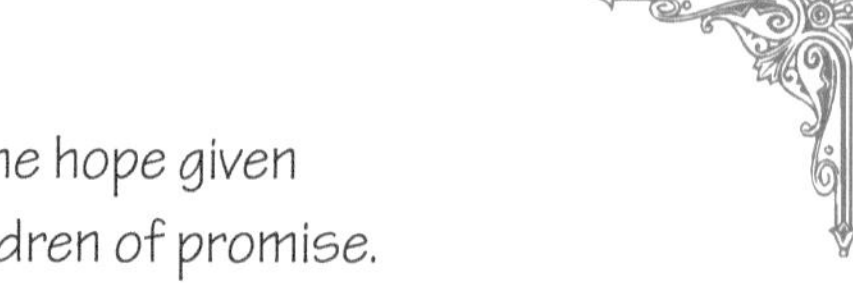

You find the hope given
To the children of promise.

So, the will to be is
A gift given to those who have
The authentic article
Of blessed assurance.

*

Passing time in a library
Of thoughts the will to be
Actualizes Truth from the scrolls
Of being in nothingness.

It is leaving the catacombs
Of thought buried in vials
Where blood spoke opening
The mystery of life
To the rhythm of the universe.

Then, the crystal crow writes
Across your heart with the blade
Of Truth and you feel life
Pour through time past.

In this living moment
Your mind awakens
To the always already there.

Then the celestial clocks chime
The advent of forevermore
And you rise from your meat.

How pure music carries you
Beyond existential
Threat of being in time
As the madness of the world
Succumbs to the authentic
Article of blessed assurance.

So, the crystal crow, your muse
Dwells in the library of your mind.

*

Feeble, sliding into silence
An old man pulls strength
From his will to be
As time wears his substance
Thin.

To fight infirmity, you stumble
Toward the light of being
Toward Truth
As your resolve drops
From weakness.

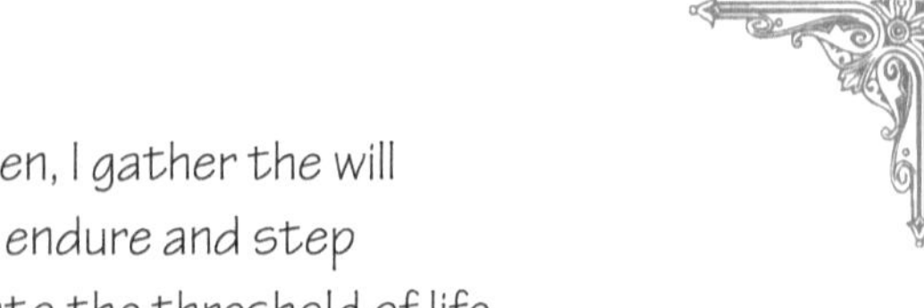

Then, I gather the will
To endure and step
Onto the threshold of life.

Leaving self-pity, you stand tall.

Then, I recall the time
Of the living moment
That built fortitude in the heart
Of being toward Truth.

There is the memory
Of the dance across thought
When the crystal crow spoke
The life of what matters
As you cherish dreams.

To fulfill purpose
Of whom I am, drives me
Onto consummating
The authentic article.

*

So, the old man looked
Through time onto space
Feeling his way through
The unknown.

There was an evil
Lurking in the shadows
Feeding his mind
With crippling thoughts.

It was that darkness was
Around the corner
And the shadows attacked
His faith.

As he held tightly to the way
The Truth and the life
His meditation brought him
To a valley of pure music
And he saw the light
Of one-dimensional reality.

Focusing his thoughts
Upon what matters
He rode the rhythm
Of the universe to
The other side of what
Was there.

Then, his will to be fed
Upon The Spirit of Wisdom.

Then the light consumed
The shadows.

*

On a cold spring day
The old man faced
His life with a chagrin
And dread filled his heart.

It was that he was challenged
By the elements and challenged
By life itself.

Then, he meditated his way
To the other side of being there
As an anthem of hope
Delivered his strength to endure.

Climbing out of defeat
He set his sights
Upon his grandchildren
And he felt the wonder
Of life.

How, day after day
Brought more promise
Of what mattered
As the rhythm of the universe
Carried him to visions
Of forevermore.

As he felt the power of life
He left his sorry bones
And soared on the love
Of The Unknown God.

So, the old man lives on
In thought, word and deed.

*

As I face absurdity
That leads
To nothingness
The void consumes
The will to be
And I knuckle under
The load of being there.

It is meaninglessness that
Confounds time and times
And a half.

Feeling my way while riding
The rhythm of the universe
I search for a means
Through this oblivion
But darkness surrounds
The living moment.

Then, you offer the deep touch.

Then, the sky opens to dawn.

Following the light
Of one-dimensional
Reality I see life blossom
As the wind of being
Toward Truth breathes
Life onto my substance.

It is through tribulation
That character is formed.

It is through facing
What is there that indwells
The authentic article.

You cannot hide from life.

*

Hit by a dream of darkness
I sink in a river of fire
And the world spins in chaos.

I feel the talons of death
Grasp my throat as life dissolves
In the belly of worms.

There is the sound of waves
Pounding relentlessly
Upon my mind
as I writhe in agony.

How desperate this feeling
As I crash on the rocks
Of oblivion.

It is only a dream
I tell myself
But the horror leaves scars.

Then, you hear pure music
Surround you and the dream ends.

Carrying your substance
To a safe place
The rhythm of the universe
Purges you of iniquity
And the light of one
Dimensional reality
Soothes your pain.

So, it is the will
Of The Unknown God
That delivers you
To the peace beyond
Understanding.

*

Although the no longer weighs
On your shoulders, the load heavy
You look to the stars reading
The language
Of The Spirit of Wisdom.

There was a time when
The majesty
Of The Unknown God
Went unnoticed but now
It is a treasure you behold.

To look onto the expanse
Of a starry night issue
The anthem of pure music
As a trumpet signals,
The beginning
Of the everlasting.

It is in the living moment
That you follow the way
The Truth and the life
As the flame of life
Flickers in the wind.

As your mind leaps
Onto the other side
Of what indwells there

Your heart feels the rhythm
Of the universe drive you
Through the unknown.

Then, you gather the light
Of one-dimensional reality
As faith, hope and love
Steer you into eternity.

*

Longing for the treasures
Of the garden
Of tables and chairs, you search
For pure music that filled
Your heart with joy.

Riding the rhythm
Of the universe, your mind
Meditates on the way
The Truth and the life
As the light of one
Dimensional reality reveals
The peace beyond understanding.

Then, you read the language
Of The Spirit of Wisdom
And the drums of eternity
Feed you with the will to be.

As a rush of thought floods
The living moment
Your mind pictures the glory
Of The Unknown God
And the celestial clocks
Explode time.

Easing into a vertical column
Of time, you gather hope
And the madness of the world
Loses its grip on your heart.

Then, you step out of the war
Of principalities.

Then, Lady Liberty leads you
To the freedom won by blood.

*

Following the breath of life
To the other side
Of being in time
You meditate your way
Through the unknown
As madness consumes
The world.

Then, images of a house
Of many mansions picture
The essential to the living moment
As your will to be serves
The Unknown God.

Then, an overture
To being in nothingness
Transfigures time
Into endless possibility.

It is the orchestration
Of time into space
That displaces the self in you
While cosmic consciousness
Of The Unknown God
Takes you to the peace
Beyond understanding.

As the will to power
Turns to ashes
You taste the freedom
Of being toward Truth.

So, you receive a clear mind
And a pure heart
From The Spirit of Wisdom.

*

Liberated by pure music
Your heart feels the deep touch
Of the always already there
As the language of The Spirit
Of Wisdom fills your mind
With wonder.

To hear the trumpet
Of forevermore as time
Rushes into eternity
Brings you closer
To one-dimensional
Reality and you picture
The domain of what matters.

Then, the mystery of life
Engulfs you in endless possibility
And your mind gathers
Purpose from being toward Truth.

Curious how the drums
Of eternity carry
The rhythm of the universe
Into your heart
As your breath celebrates
The living moment.

So, your inner eye sees
Your journey to forevermore
Through the way

The Truth and the life.

*

So, time and times and a half
Passed into the dawn
Of being toward Truth and visions
Stirred in the back roads of mind.

Then, images of the way
The Truth and the life pictured v
What matters as you
Eclipse being in nothingness.

It was a celebration of light
Over the darkness of absurdity.

It was the rhythm
Of the universe calling you.

Although the madness
Of the world defined
The landscape of being
In time, you looked
To The Spirit of Wisdom
For hope and pure music
Took you to thoughts
Of promise.

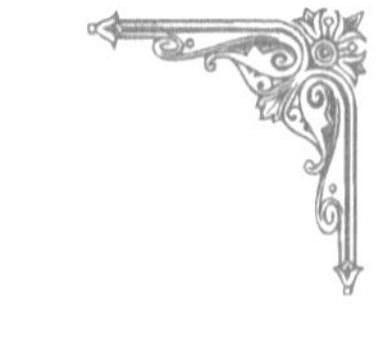

Then, the mystery of life
Opened your heart
To The Unknown God
Infusing you with
The authentic article
Of blessed assurance.

*

Dancing in the sky
The crystal crow defines
The landscape of thought
As endless possibility
Baffles the imagination.

To have been chosen to being toward
Truth is the ground of what matters
As you leap into the other side
Of being in nothingness.

It is without the creation
Of time there would be no life.

It is time that allows
Being in nothingness
To escape from absurdity
And reside in the presence
Of The Spirit of Wisdom.

Then, the crystal crow carves
Eternity into your heart
With the blade of Truth.

To know beyond the appearance
Of the here and now
You purpose yourself
Into the living moment
And the drums of eternity
Fill your thoughts with the light
Of one-dimensional reality.

So, the here and now is
Merely a theoretical construct
And the intersection of time future
And time past is consciousness
As being toward Truth
In the living moment.

*

An old man stepped to the edge
Of eternity saw that it was not
Of choosing between
Faith and the rational but
A matter of being chosen to believe
In the way, the Truth, and the life.

Then, he leaped from being there
To being toward Truth.

Then, he breathed in
Star dust brought to him
By the crystal crow.

There was the mystery of life
Taking him through the unknown
To a house of many mansions.

Although his body was infirmed
His spirit grew in power and strength.

Then, pure music took him
To the center of the will to be.

It was with a clear mind
And a pure heart that connected
Him to The Spirit of Wisdom
As he praised the glory
Of The Unknown God.

So, his being toward Truth
Found the promised land
And the living moment gave him
Life onto forevermore.

*

Meditating on the quick
Of pure music, you gather
Visions of the other side
Of the here and now
As the mystery of life
Awakens your journey
Into the unknown.

To see the face
Of endless possibility
You mold your thoughts
Through the looking glass
Of The Spirit of Wisdom
As being toward Truth takes
Your own self into a valley
Of dry bones.

Then, time bleeds Truth
As the living moment
Pyramids into what matters.

Although shadows weigh
Upon your heart, pure music
Fills you with faith, hope and love.

So, you believe yourself
Into the presence
Of the drums of eternity
That carry life and a parabola
Of time pictures forevermore.

Then, the way, the Truth
And the life trumpets you
Into being toward Truth.

*

Although linear time wears you thin
Your passion for Truth drives
Your will to be to endure.

It is the search for Truth
That conquers meaningless
As endless possibility
Staggers the mind.

Riding the rhythm
Of the universe, you see
Each day as entrance
Into the unknown
As pure music reaches
Into your heart with purpose.

Then, your substance drinks in
The authentic article and you feel
The blessed assurance given
To you by the way, the Truth
And the life.

So, Tre Spirit of Wisdom guides
Your faith, as the light of one
Dimensional reality defines
What matters.

Where reason collapses
Under its own weight
Your faith carries you
Into the presence
Of The Unknown God.

So, to conquer defeat
You feed the will to be
With faith, hope, and love
The attributes of being
Toward Truth.

SECTION 7

Living in metaphor

Although she is a vapor
A cloud before the inner eye
To see the other side
Of the here and now
You must clear your mind
With what matters.

So, you forgot the heart
Of Truth written in the stars
Of forevermore as linear time
Concealed the rhythm
Of the universe.

So, you are blind to the Truth
And deaf to your calling.

Awaken to the way
The Truth and the life
As The Spirit of Wisdom
Dwells in the living moment.

Then, she takes me out of my body.

Then, her vapors fill
My substance with the desire
To serve The Unknown God.

So, she is the crystal crow
My muse, purposing me
With what matters.

*

It is the taste of freedom
That infuses hope
As The Spirit of Wisdom
Works in the blood.

You hear the trumpet
Of forevermore pyramid
Life into the living moment.

Although you limp
In the shadows of infirmity
Your mind wrestles
With attacks
On being toward Truth.

Awakening to the way
The Truth and the life
You envision thoughts ripen
With wonder.

It is Lady Liberty shining
In the dawn
Of whom you are
As she liberates you
From captivity
Fostered by the madness
Of the world.

Hoping for your destitution
To pass, you feel the presence
Of The Unknown God
Caressing your brow
With love.

*

As the drums of eternity
Liberate you from the madness
Of the world, pure music
Surrounds you with star dust
And time in space defines
The doctrine of the landscape.

Meditating on the authentic
Article of the way, the Truth
And the life, you feel
The Spirit of Wisdom fill
Your mind with the always
Already there as The Unknown
God feeds you with blessed
Assurance.

Then, the crystal crow
Takes you inside
The living moment.

Then, visions of what
Matters purposes meaning
Into your heart.

It is the echoes of the drums
Of eternity that brings
The light of one
Dimensional reality
Allowing you to step
Out of your body.

Then, life fills the living
Moment with promise.

*

While among the stars
That fill the sky
With promise, the crystal crow
Listens to The Spirit
Of Wisdom as she delivers
The message of wonder.

She is a messenger of hope
That writes promise
Of forevermore onto your heart.

Then, eternity opens your mind
To the way, the Truth, and the life.

Then, your substance feels
Faith, hope, and love.

As the crystal crow voids
The madness of the world
You breathe the air of freedom
And ten thousand, thousand
Angels adorn being toward
Truth with the light
Of one-dimensional reality.

Guiding you through
The unknown, she
Pictures a vertical column
Of time as she takes you
To the presence of The
Unknown God
Through the looking glass
Of the always already there.

Then, you live
The meaning of life
As your purpose defines
The doctrine of the landscape.

*

As I slept, a dark figure
Appeared at my bed side

And it puzzled me.

I took it as a mystery of life.

Following me throughout the day
Thoughts of it haunted me
As I wondered what it meant.

I did not recall a voice
Merely the presence
Of this silhouette.

So, I saw it as a visitation
From the other side
Of what is there, connecting
To my sensibility.

Meditating on the figure
Drew no conclusion.

Although I felt dread
Throughout the day
I listened to pure music
And thoughts of the way
The Truth, and the life
Led me to accept the figure
As the unknown.

Dismissing thoughts
Regarding the dark figure

Drew my faith ever stronger
In The Unknown God
Through The Spirit
Of Wisdom.

It is facing the unknown
That amplifies the need
For faith.

*

In the library of mind
Where thoughts orchestrate
The way of being
In the thingness of being there
You liberate the self
From entanglements
With the web of absurdity.

As you pursue Truth
The breath of the always
Already there blows
Through your substance
And time, leaves the now
For the living moment.

This extended interlude
Takes your consciousness
Onto a level where ideas

Form pictures as a two
Dimensional reality awakens
Being toward Truth from oblivion.

Then, you read volumes
Of thought into your mind.

Following the scent
Of knowledge, you reach
The necessity of faith.

Then, your heart lives
In the mystery of life.

*

Summoning the will to be
He battled the ache
Of being there as he faced
The madness of the world.

There was a malevolent wind
Blowing through his brain
As he breathed the desire
For freedom.

Captive of pain, he
Stood in a forest of dreams
Numbering the leaves
On the trees.

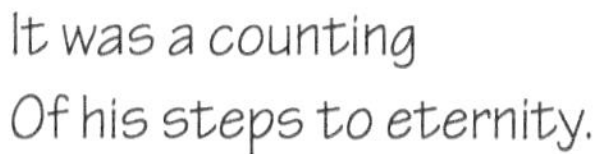

It was a counting
Of his steps to eternity.

Then, he saw the crystal
Crow glistening in the light
Of being toward Truth
And his consciousness took him
Out of himself and into the ease
Of a sweet trance.

As his mind floated
Across a sea of time
In space, he felt
The presence of The Spirit
Of Wisdom take him
Onto the other side
Of the expanse
And there, he accepted
The mystery of life
As endless possibility.

So, the ache no longer
Was a burden but defined
Time past in the madness
Of the world.

*

It is the dawn of time in space
Where mind

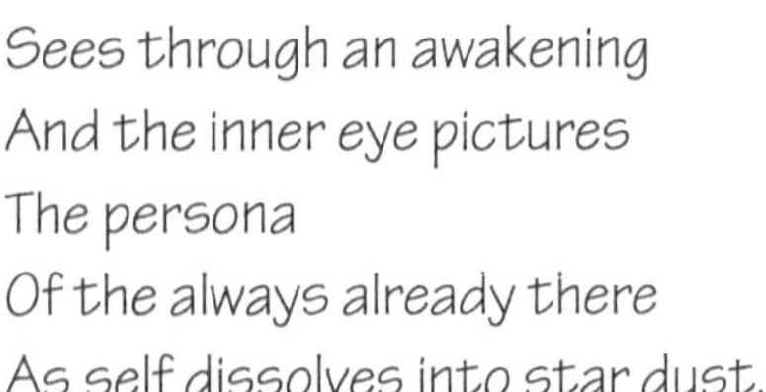

Sees through an awakening
And the inner eye pictures
The persona
Of the always already there
As self dissolves into star dust.

Reaching into pockets of knowledge
Your thoughts unscramble
The mystery of life
And you accept the unknown
As endless possibility
To be probed, a purpose
In being toward Truth.

While you stand in a valley
Of dry bones, your heart
Pounds life into the living moment
And the sky opens treasures
Of forevermore.

Then, wind chimes announce
The authentic article endowing
You with meaning as the cut
Of absurdity leaves no scar.

So, you step out of the clouds
Of being there and you overcome
The existential threat launched
By the madness in the world.

Then, your scarlet transgressions
Are cleansed
Turning them into the white of snow.

Then, The Unknown God smiles.

*

It is that cosmic consciousness
Emanates from The Unknown God
Carrying love and Truth for those
Who hears the calling.

Among the graveyards
Of time in space
Thoughts of forevermore
Rise from the ashes
Of being toward Truth.

So, you have seen
The beauty of the scarlet rose
And observed the dance
Of the crystal crow
In the sky.

So, you feel the mercy
By faith in the way
The Truth and the life.

Although philosophers, ridicule
You, you breathe the breath
Of The Spirit of Wisdom
And you are delivered
From the madness of the world.

As despots whither
In their rule, you endure
Their oppression
As you adhere to the freedom
Of your faith.

So, you have life
In the living moment.

*

Although the madness
Of the world lashes out
To consume you
Your faith in The Unknown God
Equips you
With an arsenal of Truth.

Because Lady Liberty battles
Against oppression
You lose your chains
From demagoguery.

Although evil in this world
Exists, it is no match
For the way, the Truth
And the life.

So, ten thousand, thousand
Angels wielding the power
Of The Spirit of Wisdom
Trumpet the demise
Of the despots.

It is the life of your faith
That generates courage
For your walk-in freedom.

So, the world stands in judgement
And evil perishes forevermore
As the celestial clocks
Signal the hour of your deliverance.

So, your pain has taught you Truth.

There is hope
For those in being
In nothingness
While the existential threat
Looms over their heart.

There is light in the darkness
As the dawn of being

Toward Truth awaits
The moment when need
For faith is fulfilled.

Think once, while you
Search for Truth
That the ache of being
In pain teaches you
The necessity for faith.

Although books by philosophers
Numb your mind
None deliver you onto the peace
Beyond understanding,

As hollow rhetoric
Takes your thoughts
Into a cavern
Of nonsense, you feel
The need for more.

There is the way, the Truth
And the life that delivers
You from angst, if you want
To hear the calling
From The Spirit of Wisdom.

So, open your heart to the love
Of The Unknown God.

*

The point of choice
Defines the human condition
To choose your way in life
But it is faith in The Unknown
God that is a matter of being
Chosen to the faith in the way
The Truth, and the life.

So, The Spirit of Wisdom
Works through the call
Touching your heart
And allowing your mind
To rest in the peace
Beyond understanding.

There is no choosing on your part.

Then, life explodes in wonder
And beauty surrounds you
With the deep touch.

Then, pure music dwells
In your heart
And your mind accepts
Your faith as a given.

So, you walk each day
In the mystery of life

Breathing in endless possibility
As your faith defines
Your purpose in being
Toward Truth.

*

Thinking the way to Truth
Flounders as the mind
Has limits and Truth
Dwells in the beyond.

In the wilderness of thought
Truth speaks to the substance
Of being toward Truth
As the mind spins hopeless
In the reason of the experiential.

It is by meditating
On the way, the Truth
And the life that opens
Your substance
To the beyond.

There is a calling
To faith that is beyond
Reason as the mystery
Of life encompasses
The living moment.

So, the beauty
Of the scarlet rose
Speaks to the heart
Of what matters
And the crystal crow
Dances, purpose
Into your mind.

Then, the will to be endures.

Then, you hear the trumpet
Signal entrance to The Spirit
Of Wisdom.

Then, your faith carries
You onto the domain
Of everlasting Truth
Because of the love
Of The Unknown God.

To be known, Truth
Relies on a leap of faith.

*

Crippled by the weight
Of being in nothingness

As the world smashes
Your mind, you hear the call

Of The Spirit of Wisdom
And time opens with hope.

So, you see the crystal crow
Bringing you mana
That will sustain you
Onto forevermore
And you hear pure music
Surround you with the love
Of The Unknown God.

So, you learn to accept
The way, the Truth, and the life
As your savior.

Then, you feel the presence
Of God Almighty;
Jesus Christ. His only
Begotten son;
And The Holy Spirit
The Spirit of Wisdom.

Although you hesitate
For a moment
The need for faith
Outweighs all doubt
And you call out to Jesus
To deliver you
From the madness
Of the world.

So, The Spirit of Wisdom
Quenches your thirst
Your need for faith fulfilled.

9 781959 143321